The Victorian Era

John F. Wukovits

LUCENT BOOKS

A part of Gale, Cengage Learning

Detroit • New York • San Francisco • New Haven, Conn • Waterville, Maine • London

GALE
CENGAGE Learning·

LIBRARY OF CONGRESS CATALOGING-IN-PUBLICATION DATA

Wukovits, John F., 1944-
  The Victorian era / by John F. Wukovits.
    pages cm. -- (World history)
  Includes bibliographical references and index.
  ISBN 978-1-4205-0933-5 (hardcover)
  1. Great Britain--History--Victoria, 1837-1901. 2. Great Britain--Social conditions--19th century. 3. Great Britain--Social life and customs--19th century. 4. Great Britain--Civilization--19th century. I. Title.
  DA550.W85 2013
  942.081--dc23
                                                    2012050146

Lucent Books
27500 Drake Rd.
Farmington Hills, MI 48331

ISBN-13: 978-1-4205-0933-5
ISBN-10: 1-4205-0933-0

Printed in the United States of America
1 2 3 4 5 6 7 17 16 15 14 13

Contents

Foreword

Each year, on the first day of school, nearly every history teacher faces the task of explaining why his or her students should study history. Many reasons have been given. One is that lessons exist in the past from which contemporary society can benefit and learn. Another is that exploration of the past allows us to see the origins of our customs, ideas, and institutions. Concepts such as democracy, ethnic conflict, or even things as trivial as fashion or mores, have historical roots.

Reasons such as these impress few students, however. If anything, these explanations seem remote and dull to young minds. Yet history is anything but dull. And therein lies what is perhaps the most compelling reason for studying history: History is filled with great stories. The classic themes of literature and drama—love and sacrifice, hatred and revenge, injustice and betrayal, adversity and overcoming adversity—fill the pages of history books, feeding the imagination as well as any of the great works of fiction do.

The story of the Children's Crusade, for example, is one of the most tragic in history. In 1212 Crusader fever hit Europe. A call went out from the pope that all good Christians should journey to Jerusalem to drive out the hated Muslims and return the city to Christian control. Heeding the call, thousands of children made the journey. Parents bravely allowed many children to go, and entire communities were inspired by the faith of these small Crusaders. Unfortunately, many boarded ships were captained by slave traders, who enthusiastically sold the children into slavery as soon as they arrived at their destination. Thousands died from disease, exposure, and starvation on the long march across Europe to the Mediterranean Sea. Others perished at sea.

Another story, from a modern and more familiar place, offers a soul-wrenching view of personal humiliation but also the ability to rise above it. Hatsuye Egami was one of 110,000 Japanese Americans sent to internment camps during World War II. "Since yesterday we Japanese have ceased to be human beings," he wrote in his diary. "We are numbers. We are no longer Egamis, but the number 23324. A tag with that number is on every trunk, suitcase and bag. Tags, also, on our breasts." Despite such dehumanizing treatment, most internees worked hard to control their bitterness. They created workable communities inside the camps and demonstrated again and again their loyalty as Americans.

These are but two of the many stories from history that can be found in the pages of the Lucent Books World History series. All World History titles rely on sound research and verifiable evidence, and all give students a clear sense of time, place, and chronology through maps and timelines as well as text.

All titles include a wide range of authoritative perspectives that demonstrate the complexity of historical interpretation and sharpen the reader's critical thinking skills. Formally documented quotations and annotated bibliographies enable students to locate and evaluate sources, often instantaneously via the Internet, and serve as valuable tools for further research and debate.

Finally, Lucent's World History titles present rousing good stories, featuring vivid primary source quotations drawn from unique, sometimes obscure sources such as diaries, public records, and contemporary chronicles. In this way, the voices of participants and witnesses as well as important biographers and historians bring the study of history to life. As we are caught up in the lives of others, we are reminded that we too are characters in the ongoing human saga, and we are better prepared for our own roles.

Important Dates During

1848
The Public Health
Act becomes law.

1861–1865
The United States engages
in the Civil War.

June 20, 1837
Victoria becomes queen upon
the death of King William.

1857
The Indian Mutiny begins.

1843
Charles
Dickens
publishes
*A Christmas
Carol.*

1854
Great Britain
enters the
Crimean War,
which lasts
until 1856.

1840   **1845**   **1850**   **1855**   **1860**

1837
American Samuel F.
B. Morse invents a
successful telegraph.

1851
The Great
Exhibition
opens in
London.

1859
Charles
Darwin
publishes *On
the Origin of
Species.*

1854
British cavalry
assault their
opponents in the
famous Charge of
the Light Brigade
during the Battle of
Balaclava.

December 1861
Prince Albert,
Victoria's husband,
dies of typhoid.

the Victorian Era

1877
Thomas Edison invents the phonograph.

1879
In the United States, Thomas Edison invents the electric light bulb.

1896
The Modern Olympic Games open in Athens, Greece.

1866
A telegraph cable connects the United States and Europe.

1888
Jack the Ripper murders five women in London.

| 1865 | 1875 | 1885 | 1895 | 1905 |

1870
The Education Act, sponsored by W.E. Forster, requires elementary education for every child.

1870–1871
Germany defeats France in the Franco-Prussian War.

1899
The Boer War, which marks the beginning of decline for Great Britain, begins.

January 22, 1901
Queen Victoria dies, officially ending the Victorian Era.

1869
The Suez Canal opens for traffic.

A New World

The Victorian era in Great Britain, lasting from Queen Victoria's ascension to the throne in 1837 until her death in 1901, proved to be one of the most exciting and revolutionary times in British history. Wide-ranging changes altered the way the country labored and amassed fortunes, molded how the British lived and provided the modern conveniences they enjoyed, thrust the nation's military and its scientists to worldwide prominence, and began dismantling a class system that had existed since medieval kings and barons ruled the land.

Change and a profound sense of self-assurance typified the era. At the beginning of Victoria's reign, the British population lived much the way their ancestors had in the 1700s, but by the time of her passing they had raced into the twentieth century, leaving other world powers in their wake as the nation recorded an impressive string of achievements. In 1837 most people lived in the country, rarely traveled far from home, had little education, could not vote, and transported produce and mail via horse. By 1901 the bulk of the population lived in large cities and towns, industry had replaced farming as the main occupation, subways and electric lights marked London as the sparkling metropolis of the world, education was mandatory, the vote had been granted to most males, and railroads and steamships sped the products of farm and factory to markets in and out of the nation.

Change and self-assurance went hand in hand. A belief in the ability to progress and transform society gave birth to changes that altered the way Britons lived; those changes in turn deepened the sense of self-confidence. By the middle of Victoria's reign, anything seemed possible, and no problem appeared too incomprehensible to solve. The British constructed factories and railroads, opened mines, and invented more powerful engines—and then took steps to clean up the harms that accompanied those changes. In a feverish burst of energy, one generation of British inventors and laborers laid the foundation for a new society, on which a second generation built additional improvements. They took such pride in their accomplishments that, as historian W.J. Reader wrote, by 1850 they began calling themselves Victorians, after their queen, an extraordinary step that has rarely occurred throughout history.

The Victorians were aided by the sweeping effects of industrialization, which transformed England from an agricultural economy that relied on the products of farming to an industrial nation that thrived on machine-made items. Because England sat on massive deposits of coal and iron ore, the country outpaced all European nations in switching to an industrial society and consequently became the world's leading manufacturer, shipper, and banker. Machines wove cotton and other fabrics in such great quantities that England could sell the products more cheaply, making them widely available in England and throughout the world, while railroads more speedily connected cities and transported passengers. Enormous profits bankrolled other innovations in technology and industry and enabled England to dominate the world's economic scene for much of Victoria's reign.

England's military prowess ensured that English economic strength would march on without interruption. England's potent navy controlled the sea lanes connecting Europe with all major markets, and her army basked in the glory of its vaunted 1815 defeat of French emperor Napoleon Bonaparte at Waterloo, a day that England celebrated each year.

Due to this intoxicating combination of industrial and military power, England considered it her right to amass a far-flung empire, both as a way to exhibit her frightening strength as well as to maintain her control of important sources of raw materials. Soldiers and adventurers rushed from England to India, Africa, Asia, and the Pacific islands, and by the end of Victoria's reign, the British controlled lands in every part of the globe and governed one-quarter of the world's population.

Changes at Home

Such profound alterations affected English society as well. For centuries English society was divided into a rigid system of three classes, each living a lifestyle that differed greatly from the other two. The aristocracy, or landed class, sat at the top and enjoyed the benefits of massive wealth it either inherited or gained from investments. A middle class performed tasks now attributed to professionals such as doctors, lawyers, businesspeople, or clerics, while at the bottom the working class labored on farms, in mines, or in factories.

This long-standing structure weakened during Victoria's reign. Industrialization offered new opportunities to

Queen Victoria ascended the throne of England in 1837. By the time of her death in 1901, England had transformed from a society of landed aristocracy to a modern industrial nation with a much better standard of living for more of her subjects.

amass wealth, which gave the middle class a chance to enjoy lifestyles that had once been the exclusive domain of the aristocracy. Factories enticed workers to leave farming areas and settle in expanding cities, and society began to condemn the lives of leisure that had always marked the upper class. Great differences still distinguished the well-to-do from the poor, almost as if two separate nations existed under Victoria, but as the century unfolded, more people accumulated wealth and enjoyed a better standard of living than before.

With citizens enjoying an improved way of life, more demands arose to extend the right to vote. Dating back to medieval times, the aristocracy considered it their right as the nation's landowners to run the nation, and even late into Victoria's reign many government officials could trace their family roots back hundreds of years to when a king or a queen had granted land and titles to ancestors. By the middle of the century, however, reform laws had doubled the number of males who could vote and laid the foundation for granting it to yet more males and to females.

By 1901 Victoria ruled over an England that had little in common with the one she observed at her ascension in 1837. English citizens could rightly boast of their achievements in science, industry, education, voter reform, military conquest, and literature, accomplishments that made subsequent generations of English citizens yearn for such good times.

Not often has history named an era after a single individual. Alexander the Great of Greece and Julius Caesar of Rome left impressive legacies in ancient times, and shortly before Victoria, Napoleon Bonaparte stamped his imprint on Europe. In England Victoria joined Henry VIII and Elizabeth I in so affecting the nation that when people reflect on their times, they first think of the sovereign. By the time Victoria had vacated the throne, the British people enjoyed a vastly different lifestyle than when she had ascended.

Chapter One

Technology and Industrialization

Because she served as queen for sixty-four years, the longest any monarch had reigned in British history, Queen Victoria stamped her imprint on her times. Men and women were born, passed through adolescence, entered the workforce, and died without knowing any other sovereign, and when people thought of the royal family, hers was the name that first came to mind. Actual political power had long since passed from the monarch's hands to the British congress, called Parliament, relegating kings and queens to advisory roles and confining their functions to public dedications and ceremonies. Even so, for six decades Victoria was a rock of stability in a time of rapid change, the foundation on which was erected a British empire that ruled supreme.

Queen Victoria

Victoria was born on May 25, 1819, the only child of Edward, Duke of Kent, the fourth son of King George III. She never knew her father, who died before Victoria turned one year old, but grew close to her mother. Until she became queen, in fact, the young girl slept in her mother's bedroom.

She developed into a strong person, however, as she showed the day she became queen. After the death of her uncle, King William IV, on June 20, 1837 (George III had died in 1820), the mantle fell to Victoria because William's three eldest sons, her uncles, had died and left no surviving heirs. She immediately exhibited a maturity that had been forged by tutors and a watchful mother.

"I was awoke at 6 o'clock by Mamma," she wrote in her journal that day, "who told me that the Archbishop of Canterbury and Lord Conyngham were here, and wished to see me." Victoria walked to her sitting room, still in her gown, where the two officials informed her of the king's death and that she was now the queen. She recalled, "Lord Conyngham knelt down and kissed my hand, at the same time delivering me the official announcement of the poor King's demise." Victoria had little time to collect her thoughts, but added later in her journal of the momentous day, "Since it has pleased Providence to place me in this station, I shall do my utmost to fulfill my duty towards my country; I am very young and perhaps in many, though not in all things, inexperienced, but I am sure, that very few have more real good will and more real desire to do what is fit and right than I have."[1]

Her early years proved difficult as she attempted to learn the intricacies of being queen. She tried to dispel others' notions that, because her mother had been born in Germany, she had too much affection for that nation. Fortunately for Victoria, the prime minister, William Lamb, the second Viscount Melbourne, took her under his wing and navigated her through the maze of British politics until she gained confidence. As she did, Victoria replaced what many had considered an informal style at court with a more ceremonial one that insisted on structure and proper manners.

A Queen and Her Prince

Melbourne's influence waned in February 1840 when Victoria married the love of her life, the German-born prince Albert of Saxe-Coburg-Gotha. "His beauty, his sweetness and gentleness—really how can I ever be thankful enough to have such a husband!" she wrote in her journal on the day of her wedding. "To be called by names of tenderness, I have never yet heard used to me before—was bliss beyond belief! Oh! This was the happiest day of my life! May God help me to do my duty as I ought and be worthy of such blessings!"[2]

The serious-minded Albert, called the prince consort (spouse), promoted scientific research and education, supported the arts and befriended authors, and tried to introduce reforms in universities and in the workforce. Though he was an advocate of modernizing the nation, he encountered opposition from many who had a stake in keeping things the way they were, especially the wealthy landowners and universities, as well as citizens who questioned the German's devotion to England. However, he enjoyed a strong alliance with his wife and with various prime ministers.

No English citizen could deny that Victoria and her husband succeeded in being role models for the country. Their love for each other was obvious, they were rarely apart, and the couple raised nine children. Theirs was the image of what a strong marriage should be.

Victoria's world collapsed in December 1861 when Albert died from typhoid fever. She wrote of her loss that she was "the utterly heart-broken and crushed widow of forty-two! My life as a happy one is ended! The world is gone for me!" She added that she had hoped to "grow old together" with Albert, and said that with his death, "I am on a dreary sad pinnacle of solitary grandeur."[3]

The nation mourned with her. On December 16, 1861, the *Times* of London

Victoria married Albert in February 1840. Their marriage would be one of true love and devotion until Albert's death in 1861.

wrote of Albert's death that "it is the loss of a public man whose services to this country, though rendered neither in the field of battle nor in the arena of crowded assemblies, have yet been of inestimable value to this nation." The editorial added that "the people of these islands could set up no better model of the performance of the duties of a wife and mother than their Queen; no more complete pattern of a devoted husband and father than her Consort."[4]

For the next fifteen years, Victoria refused to appear at any public function unless it was to unveil a monument erected in Albert's honor or to promote one of his causes. For the remainder of her life, she appeared only in black, the color of mourning, earning her the nickname the Widow of Windsor. Victoria's popularity dropped during these years, but once she was better able to handle the loss of her husband and reentered the public world in the 1880s, she quickly regained the devotion of her subjects and was loved for the rest of her reign.

Guided by a succession of prime ministers, particularly by the effective Benjamin Disraeli and William Gladstone, Victoria believed the British had the right and the duty to bring the benefits of civilization to uncivilized countries. She was a model of proper behavior and condemned those who failed to work hard or wasted their time in what she considered trivial matters. She opposed the attempts of reformers who argued for the rights of females, believing that women and men occupied different social worlds that should be kept distinct.

By the time of her Golden Jubilee— the fiftieth anniversary of her ascension to the throne—in 1887, Victoria was beloved throughout the nation. She reigned during a time of vast changes that saw her nation advance both at home and abroad, and she so impacted her time that the period has to this day been labeled the Victorian era.

Hope and Speed

Besides the queen herself, a sense of hope and of optimism in achieving greatness and solving problems formed the foundation of the Victorian era. Throughout much of her reign, people looked at the present as being better than the past and expected the future to be an improvement over the present. An improved society was expected, and should a problem arise as a result of technological or economic advances, scientists or doctors or reformers would provide a quick correction.

Inventors and their inventions were the role models of the day, the 1800s version of the star baseball or football player in the modern-day United States. From their fertile minds emerged the underground electric train—or subway—miracle drugs for medicine, and other creations that made life simpler and healthier.

Faster travel and communications became another trademark of the Victorian era. Before the queen ascended to the throne, the pace of travel and communications had been the same for centuries, relying on the horse for travel on land and the boat at sea. New technology yielded wondrous marvels— steam engines, railroads, steamships, and canals—that increased the speed of travel from 12 miles per hour (19km/h) in the early part of the 1800s to 50 miles per hour (80km/h) later in the century, whisking passengers to their destinations faster and in the process freeing time for other pursuits. The opening of the Suez Canal in Egypt, which connected the Mediterranean Sea and the Red Sea, eliminated the need to travel around the southern tip of Africa to reach India and the Far East and replaced it with the much shorter direct route.

In 1856 Henry Bessemer revolutionized the method of processing iron into steel by producing a lighter, yet stronger, product. This in turn led to more powerful steam engines, lighter steamships that could navigate the oceans more quickly, and improved railway tracks and bridges. Ships powered by steam engines lowered the time to cross the Atlantic Ocean to the United States from forty days at the start of the century to nine by midcentury.

Those same inventions rushed the products of farm and factory to British and world markets faster and more cheaply, turning Great Britain into the wealthiest nation and lowering the price of many items, with the result that the poorer classes could enjoy things they never before possessed. Faster ships and the newly introduced refrigeration brought fresh produce from markets as far away as Australia and New Zealand and rushed British products to those same markets.

Advances in Communications

Faster communications also included the transmission of information and messages. No longer were villagers isolated from news of national affairs or unfamiliar with life in the larger cities as they once had been. Technological advances enabled them to travel more cheaply and to see more of the country, in the process shattering the differences that separated the different parts of England and developing a sense of unity.

In 1840 the penny post revolutionized the mail system by lowering the cost of mail to a penny per half ounce (14g), no matter where in the country it traveled. This made sending mail affordable for everyone—the cost had been as much as nine times greater—moved mail much faster, and bound the country closer. The impact was so dramatic that Gladstone said, "Never, perhaps, was a local invention and improvement applied in the lifetime of its author to the advantage of such multitudes of his fellow creatures."[5] Under an avalanche of technological innovation that conquered all save the air—the airplane would not become common until the next century—regional differences eased and England became more tightly united.

In 1846 the first British telegraph company began transmitting messages in seconds from London to other parts of the nation, and within twenty years a cable laid on the ocean's floor connected Great Britain with the United States. In 1870 another cable connected London with India, making it simpler for British authorities to relay instructions to officers and supervisors in faraway possessions. A further advance occurred in 1870 when the national post office took control of the postal system and connected lines to most cities and towns. Though not a British invention, Alexander Graham Bell's telephone further helped link the nation in the late 1870s.

A Family Affair

Besides serving as the official rulers of Great Britain, Queen Victoria and Prince Albert raised a large family. The couple produced nine offspring between 1840 and 1857:

Princess Victoria	Born November 21, 1840
Prince Albert Edward	Born November 9, 1841
Princess Alice	Born April 25, 1843
Prince Alfred	Born August 6, 1844
Princess Helena	Born May 25, 1846
Princess Louise	Born March 18, 1848
Prince Arthur	Born May 1, 1850
Prince Leopold	Born April 7, 1853
Princess Beatrice	Born April 14, 1857

Victoria, who lived to age eighty-one, outlived three of her children—Alice, Alfred, and Leopold.

Queen Victoria and Albert would produce nine children between 1840 and 1857.

Amid the vast modifications, one aspect remained untouched. Standing firm, a constant in a sea of change and a link to prior monarchs, Victoria reminded her subjects of glories past, when the legendary king Arthur brought order to chaos and Elizabeth I's ships defeated the vaunted Spanish. England had been great in earlier times; in the Victorian era she was great again.

Railroads

England under Victoria developed into a world power in methodical fashion. Vital natural resources, especially the vast coal supplies mined from its coal regions in the north, fueled the steam engines that revolutionized industry and travel. Those engines powered the railroads and steamships that fueled England's rapid rise to world economic

Built in 1825, the Stockton and Darlington Railway was the world's first public railroad. Soon all of England would be linked by rail.

and military dominance. The railroads and steamships smashed the regional differences and created a more unified England. That unified England used the profits from the Industrial Revolution to amass a powerful military, which controlled the oceanic shipping lanes and grabbed possessions around the globe.

Nowhere would such rapid change be more evident than in the railroads that linked the nation and in the factories whose products brought such prosperity to England. Hand in hand, the railroads and factories changed the British landscape and ushered in new wealth and new ways of living.

The horse-dawn stagecoach was still the primary method of transportation when Victoria took her throne, even though a few railroad lines had been installed shortly before her reign began. The first passenger train, organized by George Stephenson, who developed an early steam engine nicknamed the *Rocket*, connected Stockton and Darlington in 1825. Though the machine traveled barely more than 4 miles (6km) per hour, it fascinated onlookers. Five years later Stephenson joined Liverpool and Manchester with a second set of tracks that shuttled coal and passengers between the cities. Even though stagecoach owners and innkeepers opposed railroad construction as a threat to their livelihoods, they faced a losing battle against a machine that would rapidly dominate the future. By 1838, one year after Victoria's ascension, more than 500 miles (805km) of track wove through the English countryside.

A massive expansion in railroad construction the next decade connected most cities throughout England. Within three years more than 8,000 miles (12,875km) of track linked London with other major cities, and lines reached to Scotland and Ireland. The existing mileage of track doubled between 1843 and 1848 to over 5,000 miles (8,047km), with two hundred thousand workers putting down more track every day. England's economy received a welcome boost as railroad owners looked for sturdy men to lay new track.

Engineers, businesspeople, and workers were the heroes of the moment as England witnessed a revolution in travel. Workers sweat as they dug and blasted their way through hills and meandered through valleys, doing most of the labor by hand since no mammoth machinery or bulldozers existed to move aside boulders or reshape hills. As W.J. Reader wrote, "It is scarcely an exaggeration to say that the railways of England were made with pick and shovel."[6] In less than twenty years, England's workforce created the foundation for what became the country's national railroad system. By 1890, 20,000 miles (32,187km) of track carried people to their destinations or rushed produce to city markets.

The Impact of Railroads

Contemporaries heralded the English worker for the incredible accomplishment. In 1840 a cotton printer of Lancashire named Thompson praised "the superior persevering energy of the English workman, whose untiring, savage industry surpasses that of every other country I have visited."[7] Swarms of English workers, called "navvies" after the navigators who built England's canals, living in makeshift tents and shanties, inundated the countryside to lay track. Working as teams they advanced across the land, leveling terrain and carving tunnels, and ignoring the dangers that could cause death or injury at any moment. In placing the line that connected Manchester with Sheffield, 43 miles (69km) to the east, 32 workers were killed and 540 injured between 1839 and 1845, all at a time before employee benefit programs aided injured workers.

Still they labored on, gaining accolades for so thoroughly linking the nation in a network of railroads. William Lindley, who constructed railroads throughout Europe in the 1840s, said, "The most eminent employers agree that it is strength of body, combined with strength of will, that gives steadiness and value to the artisan and common English laborer."[8]

Though travel for passengers could be uncomfortable, with people in third-class accommodations often standing in open cars, in 1850 the country's railroads carried 73 million travelers. A dispute between rival line developers, Stephenson and Isambard Kingdon Brunei, threatened to halt development when Brunei installed track 7 feet (2.1m) apart as opposed to Stephenson's 4 feet 8.5 inches (1.4m). The disparity forced lengthy delays whenever the two tracks met because workers had to switch cargo and passengers had to change

trains. In 1846 the government stepped in and began requiring all new track to conform to Stephenson's dimensions.

An earlier move toward efficiency had occurred in 1842, when the Railway Clearing House organized a national railway system that offered regular schedules and prices. Two years later a government law revolutionized the industry by requiring at least one train per day, stopping at every station along the way, on every passenger line, and offering a ticket for third-class passengers for the affordable rate of one penny per mile instead of double or triple as might normally have been charged. This farsighted move made travel about the country affordable for almost everyone, rather than only for the wealthy, and helped shatter the isolation that villagers had experienced for hundreds of years.

By the 1890s government oversight of the railroad network had been firmly implanted. Each day twenty-nine trains carried passengers from London to Manchester and back, and each day in the countryside as many as five trains ferried passengers to their destinations.

Railroads and National Unity

The great railroad boom benefited England during the Victorian era in many ways. The massive undertaking, which included the building of bridges, the laying of thousands of miles of track, and the removal of hills and slopes, opened up many job opportunities. The enterprise required engineers to draw the plans, factories to produce the track,

The British Government

Though the kings and queens of England once wielded immense power, by Victoria's time they held more of a ceremonial position and symbolized the greatness that had been England's for hundreds of years. Real power rested elsewhere. The leader of the political party holding the most seats in the House of Commons in Parliament became the prime minister, who led the nation. He kept Victoria informed of important matters during regular visits, but she had little say in his decisions. The prime minister acted in consultation with his cabinet, a group of up to fourteen men who advised him on domestic and foreign matters and helped him decide what steps to take.

The prime minister had to consult with Parliament, much as the U.S. president asks Congress to approve his requests for new laws. The upper house of Parliament, called the House of Lords, ranged from 421 to 577 members, depending on new titles granted by the queen, and the House of Commons had 658 seats until 1885, when the number was increased to 670 due to voter reform laws.

mines to yield the coal, and thousands of workers to turn the raw materials into reality. Because the railroad could take people to and from home more quickly and cheaply than previous modes of transportation could, new factories could now attract workers from 20 and 30 miles (32km to 48km) away rather than rely on a local workforce. Citizens living in London or other large centers could enjoy a more varied diet because trains rushed fresh fruits and dairy products to market before they spoiled and steamships brought goods from distant places such as America and Australia. Fish and chips—*chips* being the British term for "french fries"—became a national favorite now that fresh fish could be shipped from coastal seaports to inland markets.

More importantly, the railroads united the population and created a sense of being British rather than being from a particular region of the country. Trains brought each day's edition of the *Times* from London to country hamlets, where inhabitants devoured news about the nation and about the world, thereby broadening their horizons from what happened around their villages to what British lawmakers proposed in London or British military commanders accomplished in Africa or India. The regional customs that had prevailed since the Middle Ages crumbled as people traveled and noticed how others lived. What had once been a nation of isolated villages turned into a nation tied together by the railroad. In the early years of

Victoria's reign, a national culture supplanted loyalty to a region.

An 1851 editorial in one of England's most prominent newspapers, the *Economist*, summed up the impact that railroads had made on the nation. While giving recognition to the steamship, the editorial stated, "But this advance is nothing compared to that which has taken place in locomotion by land within the last twenty years. It is here that our progress has been most stupendous—surpassing all previous steps since the creation of the human race." The editorial added that the average speed of travel, about 5 to 10 miles per hour (8km/h to 16km/h), had changed little since "the days of Adam," but that "in 1850, it is habitually forty miles an hour, and seventy for those who like it. We have reached in a single bound from the speed of a horse's canter, to the utmost speed comparable with the known strength and coherence of brass and iron."[9] The best part of it, according to the editorial, was that the railroads benefited all classes of people, especially the poor, who now enjoyed a cheap way to travel around the country, observing new sights and experiencing new traditions.

The Comet was the first commercially operated paddle-wheeled steamship in Europe. Built in 1812, it established communication between Scotland's West Highlands and Glasgow.

Factories and Mines

Building a thorough network of railways throughout the nation required enormous amounts of coal to drive the engines and iron to produce the locomotives, freight and passenger cars, and track. This led to the rise of factories that created iron and other items, and it built a demand for coal from mines in England's coal country to the north. Widespread prosperity resulted.

Rather than obtain necessary products from thousands of workshops established in individual homes, as had been done for hundreds of years, a factory brought everything together—the workers, machinery, raw materials—needed to produce iron, cotton, and other goods in massive quantities. This more efficient system led to lowered costs of items and, through increased wages, raised the standard of living for the workers engaged in the factories.

The early factories had been small businesses, such as mills located along rivers where water-powered looms turned out cotton and other textiles. James Watt's steam engine revolutionized the industry, however, and before long, larger mills and factories appeared, from iron factories hiring hundreds of workers to smaller operations employing ten or twenty people.

Factories first appeared in the cotton and iron industries and then spread to other manufactured goods. Cotton made up almost half of England's exports soon after Victoria became queen, and by the later part of Victoria's reign, factories had completely replaced domestic industries. Sizable manufacturing centers arose in Lancashire and Manchester to London's northwest, which experienced tenfold increases in population from 1800 to 1850.

Going hand in hand with the factories were the coal mines of northern England, which operated long hours to yield the substantial amount of coal required by the railroads and factories and to heat the many homes built to house the thousands of families employed by the factory owners. Annual coal production soared from 10 million tons (9 million t) in 1810 to 100 million (90.7 million t) in 1865, then jumped to 200 million (181 million t) only ten years later. The number of coal miners increased from seventy thousand at the start of the century to two hundred thousand in 1850.

Factories and mines not only helped the nation become the world's foremost economic power, but helped the people involved as well. Though the work was dangerous, coal miners often earned among the highest wages paid to the laboring force. Although it was just a fraction of that earned by factory and mine owners, this income helped laboring families enjoy a more pleasant life style than had existed before the Victorian era.

The rapid expansion of factories and mines led to three changes in England. Beginning with the Factory Act of 1833, the government recognized a need to inspect and regulate the working conditions of private operations, which led to enormous social improvements. Secondly, by concentrating so many

Coal would fuel Britain's Industrial Revolution. By 1875 coal production had soared to 200 million tons a year produced by nearly two hundred thousand miners.

laborers in a single location, factories and mines made it simpler for unions to form. These unions battled owners for better wages and enhanced working conditions. Finally, factories became the equivalent of social centers for workers and their families, offering services not seen before. Sports clubs and bands offered workers the opportunity to be involved in something outside of work and allowed wives and children to enjoy pastimes that had once been reserved for the well-to-do.

Built on the backs of inventors, businesspeople, and laborers, the successes of the Victorian era made people proud to be British citizens. Should anyone question their pride, they had modern technological advances, cities, a worthy queen, and the Exhibition of 1851 as ready answers.

Chapter Two

The Splendor of Victorian England

The impact of the Industrial Revolution propelled England to the top position among world economic powers. That success in turn led to accomplishments in other areas. The famous Exhibition of 1851 celebrated the many achievements accomplished in the Victorian era, and the rise of London and other British cities proved that England under Victoria was unlike England of the past, when villages were the rule. In the process, however, these triumphs seriously weakened the three distinct social classes that had long marked the landscape.

The Exhibition of 1851

If anyone doubted the progress England had made since Victoria became queen, all he or she had do was visit the heralded Exhibition of 1851, which opened in London's Hyde Park on May 1. Officially titled the Great Exhibition of the Works of Industry of All Nations, since many countries sponsored exhibits, the five-month festival mostly celebrated the inventions and industries that had so dramatically changed Great Britain since 1800 and emphasized that change and rapid communications were trademarks of their times. Receiving strong support from Albert, who foresaw that the event would showcase British achievements and cast England in a positive light, the exhibition attracted 6 million visitors before it closed in October of that year.

"This day is one of the greatest & most glorious days in our lives," Victoria wrote in her journal on opening day, May 1, 1851. "It is a day which makes my heart swell with thankfulness." The queen favorably commented on the visitors' cheerful demeanor and wrote that so many people descended on Hyde Park that it was "filled with crowds as far as the eye could reach."[10]

Standing in the middle, dominating Hyde Park with its magnificence and size, stood the Crystal Palace, the world's first large structure built from steel and glass. Designed by Joseph Paxton and meant to symbolize England's wealth and creativity over the previous half century, it stretched six football fields long, was 400 feet (122m) wide and 66 feet (20m) high, and occupied 18 acres (7.3ha) of Hyde Park. Erected from identical prefabricated, interchangeable parts, the building could be easily dismantled and rebuilt.

"I made my way into the building; a most gorgeous sight; vast; graceful; beyond the dreams of the Arabian romances," wrote Thomas Babington Macaulay, a British historian and politician who served as Victoria's secretary of war from 1839 to 1841. "I cannot think that the Caesars ever exhibited a more splendid spectacle."[11]

Displaying more than one hundred thousand exhibits from thirteen thousand exhibitors from nations around the globe, the exhibition divided items into four groups—raw materials, manufacturing, fine arts, and machinery. Visitors marveled at the displays, much of which they had never before seen. They studied the factory and agricultural machinery on which England had built its recent glories, stared in mute wonder at the huge engines and locomotives, and gasped when the telegraph instantaneously transmitted messages from London to other British cities.

The Crystal Palace in Hyde Park was designed by Joseph Paxton and was built to house the Great Exhibition of 1851.

Henry Mayhew, a writer who studied England's working classes and poor, wrote that the first week or two, the carriages of the wealthy jammed the streets leading to the exhibition. Then the poorer and the working classes attended, eager to inspect the marvels of industrialization and science, especially the machinery. "You see the farmers, their dusty hats telling of the distance they have come, with their mouths wide agape, leaning over the bars to see the self-acting mills at work," Mayhew wrote. He added that around each machine "are anxious, intelligent, and simple-minded artisans, and farmers, and servants, and youths, and children clustered, endeavoring to solve the mystery of the complex operations."[12]

The exhibition simultaneously celebrated the accomplishments of businesspeople and inventors while boosting their reputations. Citizens looked to them as examples of what one could achieve through hard work, and biographies of railway engineers and scientists became popular. Eight years later Samuel Smiles published a book titled *Self-Help*, which argued that everyone, not merely the wealthy, could attain a prosperous life if they were willing to put effort and sweat into their endeavors.

The exhibition became the dividing mark between the old and the new, a sign of the promise that lay in the future rather than a glance at past glories. The *Economist* of London described the numerous changes that differentiated 1851 England from 1800 England and cited as progress that a letter that had taken one week to move from London to Edinburgh now took one day, that passengers traveled at the rate of 50 miles per hour (80km/h) rather than 7 (11km/h), that city streets were lit by brighter gas lights rather than dim oil lamps, and that a trip to the United States now took ten days in a steamship rather than eight weeks in a sailing ship. The English had turned to the railroads, steamships, and the telegraph rather than the horse and boats for travel and communications. The newspaper declared:

When we refer to a few only of the extraordinary improvements of the half-century just elapsed, we become convinced that it is more full of wonders than any other on record. Of that wonderful half-century the Great Exhibition is both a fitting close and a fitting commencement of the new half-century, which will, no doubt, surpass its predecessor as much as that surpassed all that went before it.[13]

The queen visited the exhibition several times each week, as delighted with the large crowds—an ecstatic Victoria wrote in her journal that 67,800 had attended the exhibition on June 17—as she was with the machinery and inventions. She added on July 18, "It was such a time of pleasure, of pride, of satisfaction & of deep thankfulness, it is the triumph of peace & goodwill towards all, of art, of commerce, of my beloved husband, & a triumph for my country. To

The latest in machine tools were on display at the Great Exhibition. All manner of technological achievement was on display in over one hundred thousand exhibits.

see this wonderful Exhibition which has pleased everyone looked upon as dearest Albert's work, this has, & does make me happy."[14]

The Jewel of London

The Industrial Revolution caused a decline in agriculture as more workers left the farms to seek work in the new factories that created the products customers in and out of England wanted. Because these workers required housing, large cities became more important during the Victorian era. In 1801, 80 percent of the population earned their living in agriculture and thus occupied country hamlets. By 1851, with factories

siphoning off the laboring force, that number plunged to less than 50 percent, and by 1901 only 25 percent lived in the country. During Victoria's years England changed from an agricultural to an industrial power, from a nation that resided in the country to one that crowded into cities new and old.

The Victorian era became the age of cities. London expanded from having only 4 percent of the nation's population to having 14 percent. Aided by the ease with which the railroads moved people around, between 1831 and 1851 Manchester grew from a population of 182,000 to 303,000, Birmingham from 144,000 to 233,000, and Leeds from 123,000 to 172,000. Whereas in 1801 London alone held over 1 million people, by 1851 nine cities, attractive because of the opportunities they offered the younger generation, could boast that number. Adjoining suburbs held many of the wealthy professionals who profited from the industrial age, while seaport cities catered to those who had money and to immigrants arriving in England from Ireland and other nations.

Resting on a plateau of its own was London. The census report of 1871 stated:

The metropolis of the Empire stands by itself. It is the seat of the Legislature, the primary home of justice, medicine, and religion, the theatre for the fine arts and the sciences, the great center of society; the emporium of commerce, the warehouse of England, the great port in communication with the sea. Spanning the broad tidal waters of the embanked Thames [River] with its magnificent bridges, it wants but a great number of grand public buildings to be the first Queen of Cities.[15]

London is shown in a panoramic view from 1845. Fueled by industry, the city's population expanded from 4 percent of Britain's total population to 14 percent during Victoria's reign.

London, drawing thousands of visitors to its parks, museums, and wonders, became the world's greatest city. It featured the sparkling new Palace of Westminster, more commonly known as the Houses of Parliament, anchored by the Big Ben clock tower. Railways coursed toward London from every other major city and town in England, and new track connected the capital with more locations every year. Steamships from around the world brought both produce to feed the expanding population as well as travelers eager to visit London. Businessmen from other nations journeyed to London's banks, anxious to bring back the money needed to support their own industrialization, and famed authors such as novelist Charles Dickens and poet Robert Browning regularly lived in and wrote of the city. Ten mail deliveries each day rushed correspondence about the city, and the Near East (which includes the modern-day countries of Turkey, Iraq, Israel, and Saudi Arabia) and the Far East (which includes the modern-day countries of China, Japan, and the Philippines) received those names because of their distances from London.

In 1854 work began on a subway system beneath existing city streets to transport city workers faster than the horse-drawn carriages that so clogged London's thoroughfares. That same year the first of hundreds of miles of sewers began draining excess water and refuse out of the city, while a labyrinth of pipes brought fresh water in. Department stores, with hundreds of shining articles adorning their shelves, enticed passersby as they finished their walks in Hyde Park and other locales, and new homes appeared with astonishing rapidity.

Different Neighborhoods

"If, early on a summer's morning before," declared an 1854 magazine article about London, "the smoke of countless fires had narrowed the horizon of the metropolis, a spectator were to ascend to the top of St. Paul's, and take his stand upon the balcony, he would see sleeping beneath his feet the greatest camp of men upon which the sun has ever risen."[16]

New expansions occurred in London every year, causing German author and social critic Friedrich Engels to write of the city in the 1850s, "London is unique, because it is a city in which one can roam for hours without leaving the built-up area and without seeing the slightest sign of the approach of open country."[17]

London offered a variety of neighborhoods, from the wealthy sections adorning the West End to the slums of the poor blotting the East End. Theaters, department stores, parks, and museums in the center of London made life a pleasant experience for the upper-middle-class residents who, with servants in tow carrying the results of their outings, embarked on frequent shopping expeditions. Residential areas gave homeowners a place to live apart from the financial and business districts, and railways whisked away those who preferred to live in outlying neighborhoods and suburbs. Street peddlers, many of whom were children, sold flowers, apples, and

Domestic Workers

Proof that the wealthy enjoyed a different lifestyle than the rest of the country can be seen in an 1861 listing of the job titles for the men and women who served aristocrats. Though some aristocrats did not possess the wealth or lands to afford every position, many did.

Males	Females
House steward	Housekeeper
Valet	Lady's maid
Butler	Head nurse
Cook	Cook
Gardener	Upper housemaid
Footman	Upper laundry-maid
Under butler	Maid-of-all work
Coachman	Under housemaid
Groom	Stillroom-maid
Under footman	Nursemaid
Page or footboy	Under laundry-maid
Stableboy	Kitchen-maid
	Scullery-maid

Quoted in Sally Mitchell. *Daily Life in Victorian England*. Westport, CT: Greenwood, 1996, pp. 55–56.

a hundred other items to passersby. London not only drew thousands of new residents from inside and outside England, but also saw the rise of suburbs and other towns in its proximity.

While life in London could be a grand experience for those with money, for those without, it could be far different. British politician Benjamin Disraeli said that London actually presented two separate nations: one for the rich and one for the poor. Critics pointed out that city authorities did nothing to ease conditions for the poor and instead packed them into unseemly neighborhoods out of sight of travelers and the wealthier classes.

"The low black houses were as inanimate as so many rows of coal-scuttles,"[18] wrote American author Henry James during a visit to London in 1888. While sewers provided relief in the nicer areas, residents in the poorer sections lived alongside dirty ponds littered with animal excrement and breathed horrid odors. Many people kept their windows shut even on the hottest of days to keep out the smells—or purchased oranges to aid in masking the stench.

Life in Other Cities

London was not the only urban center that experienced rapid expansion during Victoria's reign. Birmingham, to London's northwest, became known as the City of a Thousand Trades because it housed so many different small industries. According to an 1841 survey, Birmingham was the home of almost one hundred different trades, with twenty-one hundred business firms involved in those areas. "Since that time," stated a report in 1864, "many new trades, some of great importance, employing a large number of persons, have been established in the town, and the population of the town has increased in the succeeding 20 years from 183,000 to 296,000, or, with suburbs, 310,000." The report mentioned the glass industry, brass and other metal-producing foundries, weaponry for the military and sporting enthusiasts, jewelry, buttons, bricks, and other items. Birmingham bustled with so much activity that the report praised "the forest of tall chimneys which meets the eye in every direction in Birmingham, and the large new works in all parts of the town."[19]

Again, the rise of a national railroad system sparked the growth of these cities and their accompanying suburbs. A businessperson or middle-class worker could now live in a suburb, catch the morning train to his or her workplace 30 or 40 miles (48km to 64km) away, and be home for supper. It became a daily

Smokestacks dot the landscape of Birmingham, England, in the 1840s. The city became a vital manufacturing center, producing glass, metals, weaponry, jewelry, and even buttons and bricks.

workday ritual for thousands of individuals to flock to London, Manchester, Birmingham, Leeds, and other large manufacturing cities for work, then reverse the flow and return to their families in the evenings.

Life in the city differed enormously from that in the country. People living in agricultural areas tended to do most everything on their own. They harvested crops, erected barns, and performed other essential tasks. In the cities, however, people relied more frequently on each other to get things done. Specialists arose who catered to the needs of city dwellers. Rather than build their own home, people hired a carpenter to construct the house. The carpenter, in turn, relied on a baker for bread, while the baker turned to a tailor for dresses and slacks, rather than making them at home.

Store owners brought products directly to homes so homemakers would not have to leave their residences, travel to market, and carry back the food or products. Butchers and milk sellers stopped by each day to deliver needed items and sent a bill once a month for the service. In the poor sections of cities, peddlers walked the streets offering fruits, flowers, vegetables, and other goods to neighborhood residents.

Later in the era huge department stores all but eliminated household industries by gathering a wide variety of products in one store. By offering so many different items, department stores made it simpler for a family to head across town or, with the railroads making travel easier, even from city to city for shopping.

The Benefits of the Cities

While people living in the country may have enjoyed a less hectic life and may have avoided the ills of residing in crowded urban neighborhoods, they lacked the many benefits a city could offer. London, Liverpool, and other places built universities for study, museums packed with extraordinary sculpture and paintings, concert halls featuring the most popular bands or symphonies, libraries with ever-expanding numbers of books, and the best schools.

In most cities technological advances and new homes constructed from sturdier materials—brick residences quickly replaced stone and wood—appeared along train lines and subway routes. By the 1870s city regulations required flush toilets and better ventilation in homes. Aqueducts piped in a fresh water supply, and sewers whisked away unsanitary water. In the last quarter of the nineteenth century, London and other cities constructed water reservoirs, scheduled regular garbage collections, paved streets for easier transportation, introduced gas lighting, and installed electric lights in new buildings and in the homes of wealthy residents. Their compatriots in rural areas, lacking the advantages of numbers and of modern city governments, could not possibly enjoy such features without traveling to London or the nearest city.

News of the benefits of living in the city more rapidly spread to the countryside in 1840 when Parliament established a national mail service. The penny post, as it was called, delivered mail to any location within the country at the cost of only a penny per half ounce (14g). With mail affordable and simple, the volume of correspondence skyrocketed. City residents raved to family members and friends who lived in the country of the marvels of London, Manchester, and other metropolises. A son might leave the family cottage for the city and then write letters home that described the joys of residing in town.

The effects of the penny post multiplied after the Elementary Education Act of 1870 required schooling for much of the country's youth and enabled more of the population to read and write. The number of letters in one post office soared from seven thousand a week in 1873 to twenty-five thousand three years later.

Aristocrats

While improving life in diverse ways, the penny post and other accomplishments of the Victorian era proved to be factors in weakening the traditional three-tiered division of society that had earmarked English life since the days of King Arthur. For hundreds of years the aristocracy, also known as the landed gentry because they supported their lifestyle through farming and land rental, stood atop the social chain. They ranged in size from those who owned small estates of less than 100 acres (40ha) to those who controlled thousands of acres of land. In 1842 there were 562 titled families, each headed by either a duke, marquess, earl, viscount, or baron who automatically received a spot in the House of Lords.

Every British citizen knew of the fabled homes such as the Duke of Marlborough's Blenheim Castle and Warwick Castle of the Earls of Warwick, both of which featured as many as four hundred rooms and one hundred chimneys and had been in use for hundreds of years. Upon the death of the family head, the oldest son inherited land, money, and a title, which meant that the younger sons had to choose from among the military, the church, or government service for their income.

Aristocrats led lives separate from the rest of society. Residing in the same huge country estate as their forebears and waited on by armies of house servants, including cooks, governesses, maids, butlers, and coach drivers, they thought little of society's ills. They spent much of their time in idleness, attending functions in London from April to July and the remainder of the year hosting or attending parties at their country estates at which gentlemen wore top hats and ladies donned elaborate gowns. Afternoon tea became popular, and men headed for their clubs or played polo. Splendidly attired men and women attended the horse races at Ascot and boat races during the Henley Regatta in July, as much to be seen as to enjoy the sporting events.

The aristocrats assumed that they were different, and better, than those who dwelt in the middle and lower classes. Upper-class sons attended the same schools together, believed in the same principles, and enjoyed the same pastimes, such as weekend parties and

Nineteenth-century British aristocrats lived in huge country estates and spent much of their time in idle pursuits, social forays to London, and hosting and attending parties on their estates.

hunting. If they committed a crime, they were judged by other nobles instead of in a regular court, and if found guilty of murder, they were hanged by a silk rope instead of a regular rope noose.

Their schools emphasized character and proper demeanor above knowledge. Educator Thomas Arnold, the fabled headmaster of Rugby School, which had catered to the sons of the landed gentry since 1567, said, "What we must look for is, first, religious and moral principles;

secondly, gentlemanly conduct; thirdly, intellectual ability."[20] Becoming a gentleman and establishing contacts with the sons of other powerful men became the hallmark of aristocratic education, taking precedence over pure knowledge.

Even as Victoria became queen, English society accepted without question these social divisions that placed aristocrats at the top while others occupied secondary status. One's standing was determined at birth. Lord Palmerston, a prime minister and foreign secretary under Victoria, praised England's class system as one "in which every class of society accepts with cheerfulness the lot which providence has assigned to it; while at the same time each individual is constantly trying to raise himself, not by violence and illegality, but by preserving good conduct and by the steady and energetic exertion of the moral and intellectual faculties with which his creator has endowed him."[21]

As Victoria's reign progressed, however, the aristocrats' hold weakened. The spread of railroads and prosperity meant that more people had the financial means and the ability to travel about the country. The more they saw of their nation, the more they wanted to break out of the mold that had gripped England for centuries, and the wealthier some became, the more eager they were to enjoy the benefits once preserved for the landed gentry.

Starting in the 1870s, agricultural depressions and competition from the United States and other nations lowered the price of wheat and other farm produce, and refrigerated shipping brought tons of beef from Argentine and Australian pastures. As they lost income, the aristocrats saw their power slip to the rising middle class, the individuals who had banked their futures on the Industrial Revolution and technology.

Critics attacked what they concluded to be the wasted lifestyles of the aristocrats, who did nothing to help society. According to these critics, aristocrats enjoyed every benefit but fulfilled none of their responsibilities to their English brethren. Though the three social classes still existed by the end of Victoria's reign, the era had severely weakened the landed gentry's hold on British society.

The Rising Middle Class

With increased population and the wealth created by the Industrial Revolution, the rising middle class became the era's most influential group. The economic power attained from operating successful businesses, combined with voting and educational reforms, handed the middle class the influence once held by the aristocrats.

England had long become accustomed to a system that divided people into three classes—the wealthy, the middle class, and the poor. While these three still existed during the Victorian era, the appearance of factories and coal mines led to a rapid increase in the number, power, and wealth of the middle class. As W.J. Reader wrote, "The sixty years of Queen Victoria's reign were above all the sixty years of the middle class man."[22]

Nothing seemed beyond anyone's reach, if only he or she were willing to work hard. Rather than remaining among the poorer laboring class or the middle class, as had been the norm for hundreds of years, individuals could improve their status in society and enjoy success by borrowing some money, opening a firm, and then through exertion and sweat, build it into a thriving business. These individuals scorned the idleness of the landed aristocracy, who

Vacation at the Sea

As prosperity grew and as railroads offered the means of more rapid, cheaper travel to more of the population, many members of the middle class were able to afford vacations. Along the coastline, seaside resort cities expanded to offer places of recreation and entertainment for the middle-class entrepreneurs who had gained wealth off the success of industrialization. On weekends they took their families from the factories and congested cities to breathe the fresh salt air of Plymouth, Dover, and other towns located along the shore; lounge on the beaches; and enjoy time away from the demands of their occupations.

The new urban middle class vacationed at the seashore to enjoy the salt air and ocean waves in communities like Brighton (pictured) in Sussex.

spent much of their time hunting and attending parties, and replaced it with energy, education, and responsibility.

Where candidates once gained entry into a profession based on whom they knew and how connected their families were, applicants increasingly had to pass qualifying examinations to prove their worth. This opened occupations to middle-class sons, who flooded diplomatic posts in India and other overseas possessions. They also flocked to the military, which in 1871 replaced the purchase of army officer posts—thus limited to the sons of the wealthy—with written examinations. The same competitive desire that fueled the Industrial Revolution and fashioned a network of railroad tracks across England prodded other professions into opening their ranks to the most qualified, not the most connected, individual.

The emerging middle class dominated the ranks of clergypersons, military officers, lawyers, doctors, bookkeepers, government officials, shopkeepers, university professors, clerical workers, and architects. As they compiled wealth, they erected country mansions and enjoyed the same activities as the aristocrats they threatened to displace.

Some even assumed the same attitudes. In 1886 a French teacher at a London school catering to middle-class sons noticed that "in England boys begin swaggering about their social position as soon as they leave the nursery." He added, "Here are the sons of professional men, of officers, clergymen, barristers. See them pointing out other boys passing: 'Sons of merchants, don't you know!'" In turn, the teacher wrote, the sons of merchants looked at other students and scoffed, "Sons of clerks, you know!" and the sons of clerks looked at sons of shopkeepers and grumped, "Tradespeople's sons, I believe!"[23]

The fathers of these students and other businesspeople became role models for the Victorian era. They were the driving force behind the factories, railroads, and steamships. They advocated reform in government and industry and financed scientific expeditions to distant locales.

By the end of Victoria's reign, the middle class represented 25 percent of British society, compared with only 15 percent at the start. They were behind much of England's successes in the Victorian era.

The Working Classes

In 1845 Disraeli published a novel titled *Sybil, or the Two Nations*. In the book, one character mentioned that Victoria ruled "over the greatest nation that ever existed." Another asked, "Which nation, for she reigns over two." When the first character wondered what the second meant, the second explained, "Two nations; between whom there is no intercourse and no sympathy; who are as ignorant of each other's habits, thoughts and feelings, as if they were dwellers in different zones, or inhabitants of different planets; who are formed by a different breeding, are fed by a different food, are ordered by different manners and are not governed by the

A group of British stonemasons ply their craft. Masons were members of the skilled working class that included carpenters, printers, police, and merchants.

same laws."[24] The two, he said, were the rich and the poor.

Members of the working class—those who labored with their hands and lacked a decent education, unlike their compatriots in the middle class—were split into two parts: the comfortable working class and the poor. Skilled artisans who served lengthy apprenticeships before becoming masters at their crafts sat at the top. They crafted fine furniture, jewelry, and other items. Other members of the comfortable working class included carpenters, printers, police, and store owners. They enjoyed a better manner of living than earlier generations of such workers, but they lived in constant fear that old age, a serious illness, or economic depression could nudge them and their families into abject poverty. Few could count on steady employment, and many relied on short-term occupations to tide them over.

As shaky as life was for them, conditions were worse for the poor. The comfortable working class felt closer to the middle class than to the poor, who were mainly unskilled workers, street peddlers, and common laborers. They laid the railroad tracks, carved the tunnels, served in the homes of the wealthy, and operated the factory machinery. They usually resided in substandard housing in a city or the country, depending on where they worked, and enjoyed only the most meager of diets. Friedrich Engels, a German philosopher, studied English society in 1844 and concluded that England's poor "must really have reached the lowest stage of humanity."[25]

No segment of the population remained unaffected by the massive changes sweeping across England during the Victorian era. Though the alterations improved life for some, they also brought widespread suffering to others, suffering that awoke politicians and reformers to the need for regulation. As a result, conditions were enhanced for the working class and others.

Chapter Three

The Abuses of
the Era

The changes that marked the Victorian era left little untouched. Cities and country, wealthy and poor—all felt the effects. As often happens in history, improvement came with a price in benefiting some while exacting a toll on others. Factory owners reaped the benefits of increased production, but in the process displaced farmworkers, and small industries suffered. Large cities offered numerous attractions that smaller villages could not hope to provide, but they also packed thousands into substandard housing. Progress negotiates a hard bargain—one may enjoy modern conveniences, but one must be prepared to pay a price.

In the wake of this transformation, men and women who cared for the society in which they lived recognized the need to take action for their compatriots who could not. Along the way they corrected the ills of industrialization and made life better for fellow English citizens.

Problems in the City

With the massive shift in population from the country to the city that occurred between 1801 and 1851, the nation experienced problems it had never seen before. Officials faced more serious issues in managing a city of fifty thousand than they had encountered when operating a town of five thousand. Uncollected garbage, poorly lit streets, crime, and inadequate water supplies became common features that challenged the talents of politicians and reformers alike.

While the wealthier classes lived in luxurious residences, the working class faced overcrowding and poorly designed homes. As late as 1885 a government commission investigating the issue concluded that homes for the working class "are often built of the commonest materials, and with the worst workmanship, and are altogether unfit for people to live in, especially if they are a little rough in their ways. It is quite certain that the working classes are largely housed in dwellings which would be unsuitable even if they were not overcrowded."[26] Overflowing bathrooms and poor drainage from homes multiplied the problem.

Some residences could be pleasant. William Taylor, who investigated living conditions in England, visited homes near Lancashire and wrote, "I found all well, and very many respectably furnished."[27] Most working-class dwellings, however, were little more than cheap, soot-covered structures jammed next to each other in long rows along waste-littered streets. Homes became nothing more than places providing a bed and a place to escape the elements.

Owners of factories created an influx of people seeking employment, but they had little desire to invest significant sums

A family sits in their one-room London apartment in 1865. Homes of the working poor were often made of substandard materials, had poor plumbing, and were often unfit to live in.

of money constructing comfortable dwellings. In 1840 government investigators stated that the owners' intent "was not how to promote the health and comfort of the occupants, but how many cottages could be built upon the smallest space of ground and at the least possible cost."[28]

Uncollected garbage and factory emissions created a foul stench that hovered over manufacturing cities, and soot in the sky drifted onto people and structures alike. The poorest section of Liverpool was so frightful that one writer in the 1860s could not even think of another spot on earth with which to compare what he witnessed. Instead, he described it as "the nethermost circle of Hell."[29]

Mothers had to walk as much as a quarter mile to retrieve well water or river water that, because of the surroundings, was often dirty from factory soot and smelly from human and animal waste. Many, weary of the long distances required to obtain water, did not bother about cleanliness. One Lancashire worker said that because of the lack of water, he only washed his neck, ears, and face—the parts that showed to others—but never his body.

This inattentiveness to proper hygiene created a fertile ground for disease. Epidemics, including typhoid, typhus, tuberculosis, cholera, and others, strained city health services throughout the Victorian era. Poor diets left people so weakened that they lacked the ability to combat illnesses, and a lack of nutrition that occurred because poorer families could not afford better food stunted the growth of children rather than allowing them to grow to a normal size. In the 1830s cholera, a lethal sickness that could kill within two hours from violent vomiting and diarrhea, was responsible for eighteen thousand deaths in England. An 1851 census reported that only 45 percent of babies in Liverpool reached age twenty and that life expectancy in Liverpool and Manchester, two areas of rapid industrialization, was only twenty-five.

Problems in the Factory and Railroads

As if home conditions were not challenging enough, laborers faced equally difficult situations in factories. In the early part of Victoria's reign, few laws regulated factory wages and safety. Men, women, and children worked twelve-hour shifts six days a week. Each day a factory bell rang at 5:30 A.M., summoning the workers to their posts. Work commenced at 6:00 A.M., and other than breaks for breakfast and lunch, the laborers remained on the job for twelve hours, working at a steady rhythm to make certain they did not fall behind their daily quota and risk being fired. At 6:00 P.M. they trudged home, too exhausted to enjoy family and fun. By the 1870s unions had reduced the hours to five ten-hour days and a half day on Saturday, but the demanding schedule still left little time to enjoy sports or hobbies.

Conditions inside the factories heightened the discomfort. Heat sapped the laborers' strength, and chemical smells

Ironworkers ply their trade at a London ironworks in 1865. Conditions in Britain's factories were abysmal. Sixty-hour work weeks and no safety regulations gave the average worker a good chance of dying before the age of thirty.

filled the air. Tasks requiring workers to repeat the same chore hundreds of times over throughout the day numbed their senses—unlike farm chores that, while difficult, at least differed according to the time of year. The noise of machinery was so deafening that one observer wrote in 1843, "A stranger finds it almost utterly impossible to hear a person speak to him or even to hear himself speak."[30]

The lack of any protective measures in factories made them a high-risk place in which to work. Productivity, not worker safety, was paramount. Workers in phosphorous factories making matches developed flossy jaw, a painful malady that attacked the teeth, gums, and jaw. Three thousand railroad workers died or sustained injuries every year, and a government investigation in 1842 discovered that the average laborer could often expect to die before reaching his or her thirtieth birthday. Owners shrugged off the dangers as the result of worker carelessness and did little to improve conditions until they were forced to by the government.

W.A. Abram, a writer investigating working conditions, visited a Lancashire factory and observed the workers leaving the factory at 8:00 P.M. "The poor jaded wretches—men, women, and children," he wrote in 1868, "who had been kept incessantly at work, with the briefest intervals for meals devoured hastily in the rooms, from five o'clock in the morning—dragged their limbs wearily up the steep hill to their homes." He added that many were deformed, in part because they began heavy labor before their limbs had grown, and oil and grime covered their hands and faces. The young were sickly, pale, "and all so evidently dejected in spirit, seemed to my young eyes the very embodiment of hopelessness,"[31] Abram wrote.

Titus Salt

Titus Salt was a man ahead of his time. At a time when most factory workers lived in shabby homes that were little more than hovels, in 1850 the wealthy wool manufacturer laid out Saltaire, a community of 150 houses adjoining his mill near Bradford. Each home had a parlor and kitchen, two or three bedrooms, and a backyard. In addition, Salt constructed a church, a hospital, and a local school for the inhabitants. As Salt's mill prospered, his community grew. By 1876 Saltaire housed eight hundred people. When asked why he provided for his workers in such fashion, at his own cost, Salt answered that he simply wanted to do what was right.

Titus Salt's Saltaire textile factory in Bradford, England, became a model for other factories. Nearby for the workers were well-built, comfortable homes, shops, and a library.

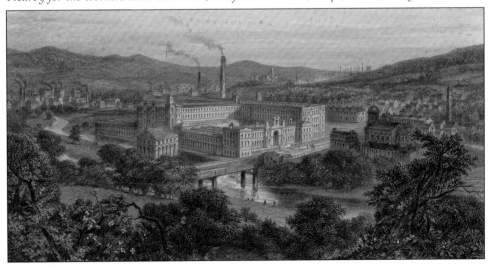

The factory's most grievous harm may have been what it did to the family. Before industrialization placed hundreds of workers under one roof, most families worked at home as a unit, either laboring on farmlands or making items to sell to neighbors. Now the fathers, sons, and sometimes the daughters left for the factory, frequently heading to different locations and often spending more time at their places of work than at their homes.

In 1841 a vocal critic of factories, William Dodd, visited a Leeds factory and wrote that the "dense clouds of smoke" all but obliterated the factory chimneys. He referred to "the many marks by which a manufacturing town may always be known, that is, the wretched, stunted, decrepit, and, frequently, the mutilated appearance of the broken-down laborers, who are generally to be seen in the dirty, disagreeable streets; the swarms of meanly-clad women and children, and the dingy, smoky, wretched-looking dwellings of the poor." He added that while a few people accumulate astounding fortunes, there were also "hundreds of thousands of human beings huddled together in the attics and cellars, or crawling over the earth as if they did not belong to it."[32]

Problems in the Mines

Factory conditions shocked reformers, but they paled in comparison to what workers of all ages faced in the mines. "No one, perhaps, would dream of making an excursion for pleasure to this great district of subterranean darkness and superficial blackness," wrote J.R. Leifchild in 1862 in beginning his dreary assessment of England's coal country in the north as part of his assignment for a magazine. He continued that even before one entered the mines, the area was "dense with houses which swarm with population, and clouded with the soot and smoke of many a manufactory." When Leifchild descended to the mine shaft in an iron cage, he made certain he kept his elbows, hands, and fingers close to him to avoid being cut by rocks. After the four-minute descent, he required another five minutes to adjust to the lack of light. When his eyes refocused, he watched the miners work in confined areas he described as "the coal-getting localities, the scenes of suffering, and the sources of pay and wages." At the end of a long day, the men dropped their pickaxes and other tools and shuffled to the shaft, "to that little circle of light which, like a fairy ring, lies brightly upon the black coal floor,"[33] for the ascent from the mine. They emerged covered with dirt and dust, their white teeth clashing with blackened faces and lips. They shuffled from the mines to soot-blanketed homes, where the stench from garbage and the depressing air overwhelmed the few green plants that broke the numbing bleakness.

The men, women, and children who labored in the mines faced hardships that weakened even the sturdiest of individuals. Poorly designed headlamps provided little illumination, and inadequate ventilation brought only brief bursts of fresh air. Coal dust that clogged nostrils

The working conditions in British coal mines were so bad from 1850 to 1914 that a thousand miners died in them every year.

and filtered into lungs produced deadly diseases. Miners worked in areas partially covered with water and faced death or maiming from falling rocks or onrushing water that burst through newly opened crevices. Most miners accepted that, if they avoided death or injury, because of arthritis and other crippling maladies, they would rarely find work after age forty.

Death was always present. One thousand miners died annually between 1850 and 1914, and each year 20 percent sustained serious injuries. In 1862, 204 miners perished in a shaft collapse at one

mine, and sixteen years later another 269 died in a similar tragedy. When a miner was trapped, the others dropped their tools and hastened to his or her rescue, and when one died, his or her compatriots mourned the tragedy as if they had lost a family member, proving to Leifchild "that the human heart can feel as warmly a thousand feet underground as in the most refined and cultivated circle of society."[34]

They mourned, and then returned to the same mines that were the cause of so much grief. A government report concluded that most adult miners expected

Inside the Mines

Working conditions inside coal mines offered some of the harshest circumstances in England. Writer J.R. Leifchild visited different sites in doing research for an article he wrote in 1862, explaining that men worked in small groups in different niches deep below the surface. Though he knew that four hundred men worked in the various side passages, he only saw three to five at a time.

Men called putters or pushers, who dragged the baskets of coal to be hoisted to the top, "creep, and drag, and push" the coal inside narrow places. Other men called hewers worked in small corners "full of floating coal-dust, foul and noisome with bad air and miscellaneous refuse and garbage," while three or four candles or a couple of lamps gave a glimmer of light. One man, Leifchild noticed, was practically naked, lying on his back and lifting a small pickax above his nose to chip away at the coal above.

Quoted in E. Royston Pike. *"Golden Times": Human Documents of the Victorian Age.* New York: Schocken, 1967, pp. 68–69.

early deaths, due to either injury or disease, and that the miner "slips into the grave at a comparatively early period, with perfect willingness on his part, and with no surprise on that of his family and friends."[35]

Work in the Country

By the middle of the century, even though agriculture lost many laborers to the factories and mines, 1.2 million men—one-quarter of all male workers—and 143,000 women tilled the fields. Their numbers slowly dwindled for the rest of the century, drawn to better opportunities in the expanding cities and busy factories, but the remainder labored and resided where they and their families had for

hundreds of years. Some lived fairly well, enjoying pleasant cottages on good farmland, but many lacked much more than the necessities. They worked as a unit to bring in the corn or wheat and tend to the animals. Men did the heaviest work and harvested the crops, women and teenagers collected and loaded it onto wagons, and the young and the old gathered the grain left behind, removed rocks from the path of plows, and shepherded animals.

They worked long days in all kinds of weather and developed ailments that sapped their energy while earning barely enough to make it from week to week. Many died in poverty or fled to factories. Some farmworkers lived in simple cottages with walls so flimsy that the winds howled through cracks, and families of all sizes made do with two rooms. They supplemented their diets with vegetables grown in individual gardens and wore the same clothes long after they had worn thin. One historian of the time, William Johnston, wrote in 1851 that farmworkers "accept labor and sorrow, overcrowding and unhealthiness, as their destined portion."[36]

As harsh as it could be for farm families, conditions were worse for any laborers they might hire for assistance. Laborers lived in stone or thatched hovels that provided inadequate shelter from wind and rain, and these individuals lacked knowledge of anything beyond the boundaries of their daily lives. One journalist of the time, William Howitt, wrote in the first decade of Victoria's reign that farm laborers "are mighty useful animals" who possessed no more knowledge than needed to accomplish their tasks and that the typical laborer "sees no newspaper, and if he did, he could not read it." Howitt added, "The worker is as simple, as ignorant, and as laborious a creature as one of the wagonhorses that he drives," and "is as much of an animal as air and exercise, strong living and sound sleeping can make him, and he is nothing more."[37]

Whether enjoying life on the farm or living day-to-day from the wages earned as a farm laborer, the future and economic well-being of all depended on one factor no one could change—the weather. A proper mixture of sun and rain would yield bountiful crops, while drought or too much rain could bring hard times. One Monmouthshire farmer wrote in his diary on December 31, 1879, "Being the last day of the year which is a very good thing it is. This year 1879 has been one of the wettest years any living man can remember and a very disastrous one for agriculture. Having a very bad yield of corn & sheep rotten & doing very bad."[38] All the farmer could do was hope that conditions improved the next year.

Child Labor

More tragic than the plight of farmworkers was the predicament faced by the thousands of children, some as young as four years old, who labored in factories, descended deep into the earth to mine coal, or prowled big city streets peddling a variety of goods. "This young woman looks very pale and delicate, and has every appearance of an approaching decline," wrote Dodd in 1841 of a teenage factory girl in Manchester. Dodd informed his readers that the young girl awoke at 4:30 A.M. and started work an hour later. A breakfast break occurred at 7:30 A.M., but not until after she cleaned the machine at which she was stationed. After the brief pause, she returned to her post and completed the same repetitive task hundreds of times over until noon, when she again cleaned the machine before receiving a break for lunch. Work resumed at 1:00 P.M. and lasted until 7:00 P.M., when she cleaned her machine for the third time. The girl then joined the other weary workers, some younger than herself, and walked home, where, as Dodd wrote, she "throws herself into a chair exhausted. This is repeated six days in the week."[39]

Factory labor offered hardships beyond fatigue and long hours. Children were maimed from operating the machinery, which inflicted injuries ranging from cuts and gashes to mangled arms and legs. Supervisors scolded or beat them if they slackened their pace, and phosphorus in match-producing factories caused severe disfiguration. Textile factory owners hired small children because they could squeeze into places adults could not and could be paid less than adult workers. Some factory owners emptied local orphanages to fill their work needs, erecting dormitories as sleeping quarters for the youth.

At different mines children opened and closed vents to bring fresh air to the workers belowground. Others wrapped wide leather straps around their waists, connected the accompanying chains to coal-laden wagons, and pulled the devices through darkened passageways to ladders that lifted the coal to the surface. All the time, no matter the task, they inhaled the ever-present coal dust that blackened their hands and faces

Children carry clay on their heads in a brickyard in 1871. Children worked long hours for a pittance, were maimed or killed by machinery on a daily basis, and were driven mercilessly by taskmasters who worked them to exhaustion.

and settled in their lungs. Seemingly endless twelve-hour days of crawling through cramped spaces in the tiny mine shafts left children haggard and bent over. Others remained above-ground, snatching rocks and other refuse from the coal. One mine worker explained to government inspectors, "I went into the pit at seven years of age, where I [pulled wagons] by the girdle and chain. The skin was broken and the blood ran down."[40]

Other children remained at home rather than leave for the factory or mines, but they produced toys and other items for their parents in conditions that could sometimes be as harsh as the factories. One girl who made gloves at home said that her five-year-old sister was already an expert at her craft. "Little children are kept up shamefully late,"[41] she added, explaining that some friends had parents who tied them to their posts and slapped them if they dozed off.

Mayhew's Children

On the streets of London and other major cities, young girls and boys hawked items such as vegetables and flowers to passersby or offered their services in sweeping manure from people's paths, holding horses, or carrying messages from office to office. As many as ten thousand children could be seen plying London's streets by day, seeking a few coins to help them and their families.

Henry Mayhew, who investigated the plight of London's poor, wrote of two orphaned flower girls, one fifteen and the other eleven. Poorly clothed and barefoot, the pair lived in a room lit by one candle. In the middle of the stark room rested a solitary bed, in which the sisters and their thirteen-year-old brother slept, separated from a married couple by a thin curtain. The trio subsisted from the earnings of what they sold on the street. "We live almost on flowers when they are to be got," said the older girl. She added that they never knew who their father was, and that their mother died seven years ago, leaving the three to fend for themselves. "I've got myself, and my brother and sister a bit of bread ever since, and never had any help but from the neighbors. I never troubled the parish [for charity]."[42]

Even worse off were the chimney sweeps. To prevent soot from building up inside the chimneys of residences and igniting, which could spread a dangerous fire throughout the house, young boys squeezed into soot-covered chimneys and brushed off the substance. Scraped and bruised knees and elbows were common, but should a boy try to turn back to mend his wounds, a cane-wielding supervisor forced him back inside.

As part of his thorough investigation into London's poor, Mayhew interviewed a fourteen-year-old chimney sweep who lived in a house with other chimney sweeps. Because of their labor inside chimneys, "The inside of the house looked as dark as a coal-pit," wrote Mayhew. "There was an insufferable smell of soot" and "every person and every thing which met the eye, even to the caps and gowns of the women, seemed as if they had just been steeped in Indian ink." The boys told Mayhew that they climbed down into the flues, often with elbows and legs spread out and feet pressing the sides to avoid plunging to certain injury or death. At the same time, they faced being trapped if they squeezed into perilously narrow spots. "I never got to stay stuck myself," one boy told Mayhew, "but a many of them did; yes, and they were taken out

Because of their size many children were forced to work as chimney sweeps. The conditions were deplorable, with many children suffering scrapes, bruises, and injuries from falls, as well as lungs filled with black soot.

The Pickpocket

Henry Mayhew often spent time with the poor children who roamed London's streets, gathering and publishing their stories to bring their plight to the nation's attention. In one account, he related the story of a fifteen-year-old pickpocket whose father had died five years earlier and who did not know the identity of his mother. Forced to make it on his own, he wound up in prison thirteen different times, where he suffered beatings and mingled with hardened criminals.

The boy said that in prison he learned how to pick pockets, mainly because the other inmates scorned anyone who was imprisoned only for begging. "So a boy is partly forced to steal for his character. Every time I came out harder than I went in," he told Mayhew. "I can pick a woman's pocket as easy as a man's, though you wouldn't think it."

He sometimes found a bed at one of London's shelters, but life inside the shelters was not desirable for many youths because, as the boy related, "they meet there with boys such as me, or as bad, and the devil soon lays his hand on them." At Mayhew's request, the boy picked his pocket, "and so dexterously did he do his 'work,'" Mayhew wrote, "that though I was alive to what he was trying to do, it was impossible for me to detect the least movement of my coat."

Quoted in Peter Quennell, ed. *Mayhew's Characters*. London: William Kimber, 1951, pp. 115–118.

dead. They were smothered for want of air, and the fright, and a stayin' so long in the flue."[43]

Mayhew learned that when the boys grew too large to fit inside chimneys, they lost their jobs. Others were replaced when companies began using machinery instead of boys to clean chimneys, which left the boys little recourse but to turn to thievery and petty crime or join the navy and head to the sea.

Despite facing an array of health concerns, in the days before government regulation, children received few days off. They worked, or they lost their jobs. At a time when they might have enjoyed the world of play that most children should experience, they filed through factory doors or disappeared into the dark mines below to help earn a few pennies for their families.

As the Victorian era rolled on, an increasingly large number of citizens began criticizing the government for allowing such abuses to exist. The working classes, which were most affected by the excesses caused by industrialization, added their voices to the clamoring for change but lacked the resources to do anything about it.

Authors and social critics took up the cry for those on the lower rungs. Attacking the abuses of the era in books and news articles, they demanded improved wages, better living conditions, and government intervention. Why, they asked, should some citizens live in squalor while a select few, the aristocracy and the well-to-do portions of the middle class, lived in splendor? The unrest that reverberated through society led to a series of reforms during the nineteenth century that reached into every corner of life and left England vastly altered from the time Victoria first sat on the throne.

Chapter Four

Victorian Era Reforms

In the years immediately preceding Victoria's reign, few citizens or groups looked to the government to change society. Since most believed that the government had no right to interfere in commercial or social concerns, a climate existed in which landowners and businesspeople enjoyed great freedom in creating their enterprises.

If anything, the government came down on the side of the owners. A law in 1799 illustrated the point by making it a crime for workers in any industry to organize in an effort to gain improved wages and benefits. The government and owners of factories and mines believed that if a person worked hard, God would reward him or her with riches and a comfortable lifestyle. Conversely, many believed that because God would punish anyone who did not work hard, the poor deserved the bleak lives they endured.

However, the demand for reform had been simmering beneath the surface. Once a few determined individuals and groups, bolstered by the writings of noted authors, turned the nation's attention to the shortcomings, the demand sparked a series of changes.

Impetus for Reform

In Victoria's early years, this desire for reform gained strength as various groups and individuals took aim at the ills that beset English society. The concentration of workers in factories and mines made it harder to ignore the harsh conditions they faced, which was easier to do when work had been dispersed among small domestic firms scattered throughout the country. That same concentration also made it simpler to unionize the workers, because so many worked under the same roof or in the same mine.

Other forces coalesced around the sentiment for change. Religious groups emphasized that the clergy, rather than simply giving sermons every Sunday, had an obligation to offer solutions for the problems of society. As a result, more ministers argued against the slave trade, favored eliminating public hangings as punishment for crimes, and claimed that child labor was an affront to civilized societies. They formed charities to assist families in need and put pressure on politicians to vote for reform laws.

As the right to vote gradually expanded to include the middle class and an increasing number of the working class, people from those groups joined in on reform efforts. With their powers growing due to the middle-class wealth from industrialization and a corresponding importance in political affairs, they applied pressure on the government and their fellow citizens to take a serious look at the issues facing society. Sentiment for laws correcting the issues became more common.

Writers—including famous authors like Charles Dickens—and newspaper and magazine reporters wrote of the need for reform. "My earnest hope is that the book may serve to give the rich a more intimate knowledge of the sufferings, and the frequent heroism under those sufferings, of the poor," Henry Mayhew wrote in his book *London Labour and the London Poor* about the poor and the street children of London. He hoped that his book might encourage those in power to work "to improve the condition of a class of people whose misery, ignorance, and vice, amidst all the immense wealth and great knowledge of 'the first city in the world,' is, to say the least, a national disgrace to us."[44]

Dickens made workers, orphans, and young street peddlers the centerpieces of his novels in hopes of making his fellow citizens aware of the problems industrialization brought. His 1839 novel, *Oliver Twist*, stunned readers with its vivid portrayal of slums and the conditions that plagued London's poorer children and prodded the government into taking action to improve the slum areas.

With each article and book, Parliament faced increasing pressure to take corrective steps. Government commissions sent investigators to study factories, mines, and slums; these investigators then wrote blistering reports condemning the ills they uncovered. Opposition from the landed gentry, who stated that the government had no right to interfere with the established system, slowly waned in the face of the rising clamor for reform.

Early Reform Steps

The 1830s and 1840s saw the government take its first steps to regulate industries. An 1833 law banned the employment of children under nine years old in textile mills and limited the work week for those under age twelve to forty-eight hours. Government inspectors, armed with the power to impose fines, visited factories to make certain the law was followed. Parliament extended the law to coal mines nine years later, and in 1847 another regulation limited the amount of time that women and children could work each day to ten hours. The next year a public health act targeted poor city conditions by requiring sewer systems and clean water in the poorer neighborhoods and the establishment of public washhouses so that anyone could clean themselves. These laws addressed only a handful of issues and left many undesirable conditions in place, but they established the principle that the government had the right and the duty to provide for the welfare of the nation's citizens.

Charles Dickens made workers, orphans, chimney sweeps, and young peddlers the centerpieces of his novels. His vivid portrayals of the plight of London's poor prodded the government and concerned citizens to push for major reforms to improve working conditions.

In another important step, in 1849 the government abolished a tax that had long been imposed on grain brought into the country from other nations. The law had been implemented to prevent the price of corn and wheat, basic staples of the working-class diet, from dropping, which protected large British landowners but took sorely needed money out of the pockets of the less fortunate classes. Two politicians, Richard Cobden and John Bright, attacked the selfish interests of the landed gentry and argued that the tax had to be repealed in the interests of the entire nation. When the law was abolished after five years of hard effort, Cobden wrote to his wife, "Hurrah! Hurrah! The Corn Bill [repealing the tax] is law and now my work is done."[45] Cobden's delight showed the importance he and other reformers attached to the government's acting on behalf of the welfare of its citizens.

A flurry of reforms occurred from 1868 to 1880 while William Gladstone (served 1868–1874) and Benjamin Disraeli (served 1868, 1874–1880) were prime minister. Responding to the people who placed them in power—the rising middle class and the rapidly enlarging electorate—they oversaw improved levels of housing safety and standards; better working conditions for men, women, and younger people; wider acceptance for unionization of workers; and more attention to health issues. For instance, in 1871 the Trade Union Act handed workers the right to organize for better wages and conditions. Four years later Disraeli shepherded through Parliament the Sale of Food and Drug Act, which ensured increased sanitation in food preparation; an Artisans' Dwelling Act, which allowed local governments to purchase and tear down slum areas to rebuild better neighborhoods; and a Public Health Act, which attempted to combat cholera, typhus, and other diseases with better sewage and sanitation measures.

The Children and the Poor

Reformers and authors especially targeted child labor as a focus of their efforts. Dickens and Mayhew were only two of numerous critics who wrote about the shame of a nation that built an industrial empire, in part, on the sweat of young boys and girls. In the 1860s a government body, the Children's Employment Commission, found that eleven thousand children worked "under conditions which undermine their health and constitution."[46] Parliament responded by regulating first the textile and mining industries and then gradually bringing other industries under its supervision.

The government also took steps to make education mandatory for all children, which, when fully implemented, would eliminate child labor. Before Parliament adopted such measures, many children either preferred work to education or had no choice. As one boy explained to inspectors, using words that reversed what should have been the norm for children, "When I am not at work I do not often get bread and meat for dinner. I had rather work than play, you get the most victuals [food] when you work."[47]

Local Government

At the beginning of Victoria's reign, local governments had more of an impact on daily lives than Parliament. The basic unit of government was called the civil parish, which was responsible for the roads, the poor, and preserving some semblance of order. A man called the justice of the peace served as judge and, as such, was the most important man in the parish.

With the rapid expansion of major cities and factories, Parliament became more vital. No longer could local government deal with issues that reached outside its boundaries and affected other locations, such as railroads running through the parish into adjoining parishes, inspections of factories that hired workers from different towns, and other matters.

One area the government never successfully attacked during the Victorian era was the plight of the poor. Laws and government programs designed to assist them helped to some degree, but the impoverished mainly turned to religious groups and individuals for help. The Poor Law Amendment Act of 1834 set up workhouses where those requiring assistance for their families could work for food and housing, but the deplorable conditions at the workhouses condemned them to failure. The government often split apart families, sending the father to one location and his wife and children to another, and it purposely offered lower wages than the poorest workers received outside the workhouses to discourage people from depending on government assistance.

Husbands found the experiences so humiliating and devastating to family unity that they resorted to any measure, even outside the legal system, rather than opt for a workhouse. Many lived in one of London's parks with their families during the day, and then shuffled to the streets at night when the parks closed. A fortunate few scraped together enough money to move to the United States or Australia, where they worked until they raised the funds to bring their families to join them.

Orphanages did their best to help children without parents, but the number of children seeking help far outpaced their resources. The orphanages often taught children a trade or how to be a servant for the wealthy so they could stand on their own, but by the end of the century much work yet remained to be done in this area.

Voter Reform

The rapid change brought to the nation by the Industrial Revolution also affected the voting system. For hundreds of years the belief persisted that the aristocracy, because they owned land and thus had greater interest in government than those who did not own land, had both the power and the right to govern. This idea, however, lost credibility as more individuals, especially the middle class, gained wealth with the vast changes sweeping the nation. People questioned why a few wealthy landowners should have so much power in government and should control Parliament when businesspeople, bankers, and workers did so much to benefit the nation. When Victoria first came to power, the ten southern counties in England held as many representatives in Parliament as the other thirty but contained only one-third the population. Although aristocrats were well represented in Parliament, industrial centers such as Birmingham and Manchester, as well as the working class, lacked representation.

The situation could not last long at such a revolutionary time in British history. Social critics attacked aristocrats for contributing little to society and criticized Parliament, especially the House of Lords, for not representing the true interests of the country. Though the House of Lords had 560 members, 90 percent rarely attended the formal sessions. The famous Victorian-era opera-writing team, W.S. Gilbert and Arthur Sullivan, described the House of Lords in one opera as a group of males who "did nothing in particular and did it very well."[48]

The first step in extending the right to vote occurred a few years before Victoria's rule when the Great Reform Bill became law in June 1832. While it did not grant the right to vote to every individual, it was a first step toward full representation—it doubled the electorate (the number who could vote) by adding 1 million new voters. It stated that aristocrats, males who owned city buildings that yielded approximately sixteen dollars in annual rent, and male farmers whose land produced the same amount of produce each year could now vote.

This law handed increased power to the middle class but left the working class excluded from representation. While the House of Lords would remain the exclusive domain of the aristocracy, the middle class took control of the House of Commons.

Workers Seek Rights

The working classes objected to being left out of the ranks of voters. They argued that they provided the labor that ran the railroads, operated the factory machinery, and mined the coal—all of which drove the Industrial Revolution—yet reaped few benefits. In the 1830s and 1840s the Chartist movement—named after a charter of freedoms its members demanded—became the first large-scale action seeking rights for workers. The Chartists produced the People's Charter, which sought annual elections to Parliament, voting rights for every adult male, an end to land ownership as a requirement for membership in the House of Commons, voting by secret ballot, the establishment of electoral districts that represented every part of the country, and the granting of salaries for Parliament so that one did not have to be independently wealthy to seek office. In July 1839 the group delivered a petition to the House of Commons that bore more than 1.2 million signatures, but it lacked the political backing of enough powerful supporters. Though the Chartists failed, they had planted the notion that the working class was entitled to the vote.

The Chartists had also found a few friends in British political circles. Disraeli introduced the Reform Bill of 1867, which extended the right to vote to every householder, all lodgers who paid at least sixteen dollars a year in rent, and farmers who owned land producing at least eight dollars in annual income. The act doubled the size of the electorate. Most middle-class males and the wealthiest of the working class could now vote.

Gladstone, whose tenure as prime minister saw so many bills become law that it was called the Great Ministry, introduced reforms throughout government and society. His Ballot Act of 1872 provided for secret balloting during elections, thereby abolishing the previous practice of requiring all voters to announce their choices. Gladstone made positions in civil service and the military dependent on competitive examinations,

Chartist demonstrators in 1848 address a crowd on the need for voting rights for the working class. The Reform Bill of 1867 finally extended voting rights to householders, renters, and farmers, effectively doubling the size of the electorate.

rather than awarding the job according to whom an applicant knew.

As the working class grew in size and unity, it gained more rights. In 1884 a reform bill granted the right to vote to most males and removed the necessity of owning land to be elected to the House of Commons. The next year another law increased the number of representatives in the House of Commons and rearranged the districts so that each contained about the same number of voters. All that remained was to grant the same rights to another large group of citizens—the nation's females.

Females Want the Vote

British females had to overcome an added obstacle not faced by their male counterparts—that they were legally dependent on their husbands or fathers. In marriage a woman had no legal rights; she and her husband were considered one person in the eyes of the law. Anything she inherited became his by right, the family resided where the husband chose, a wife could sign no legal contract and, in the case of divorce, could not count on gaining the custody of their children.

In the late 1840s, about the same time the Chartist movement agitated for the rights of males, the first organized actions on behalf of females appeared. Women sought the right to an education and to enhanced employment opportunities, which had been severely restricted to governesses, maids, and a handful of other occupations. They hoped to enjoy the benefits gained by middle-class males and sought employment as clerics, bookkeepers, and other positions.

Agitation through the years produced results. The Married Women's Property Acts of 1870 and 1882 gave women control over what they earned and allowed them to retain anything they inherited. As more avenues opened for females, they began to ask for additional rights.

Domestic work as maids and servants provided, even at the end of the century, the largest source of work for females, but opportunities in other areas made such work less appealing. Jobs in factories, as seamstresses, and in clerical work gained popularity. The invention of the typewriter and telephone in the 1870s created thousands of openings, filled mostly by women, and in 1876 women were licensed to practice medicine. Nursing schools and social work provided new opportunities, and universities began accepting females. Though females did not gain the right to vote until the next century, the early steps toward equality were taken during Victoria's reign.

British Education

Little of the progress that unfolded in the Victorian era would have occurred without a corresponding transformation in education. In Victoria's early years as queen, children often grew to adulthood without having any proper schooling, but education reform in the second half of her reign made education mandatory. The benefits of education opened new worlds for younger people, who saw opportunity and excitement where dreariness and empty futures once existed.

Public school elementary education for all children was rare until the 1870s. Most towns relied on charitable organizations or religious groups to instruct their children. The 1841 census showed that less than 10 percent of working-class children had gone to school for more than two or three years, and ten years later only about 40 percent were even in school.

Aristocrats and the wealthiest of the middle class often turned to governesses or tutors to prepare their children for advanced education in the public schools, which existed to educate boys from wealthy families. Institutions such as Eton, Harrow, Rugby, and St. Paul's focused on loyalty, honor, and service at the expense of a rigid curriculum until the headmaster at Rugby, Thomas Arnold, implemented revolutionary measures. While retaining the emphasis on character and service, he grouped the students at Rugby by ability and added courses in science, history, literature, and foreign languages in the hopes of better preparing the men who might one day run the country.

Besides these public schools, which were more like exclusive institutions for the wealthy, other forms of instruction educated children. In the country, a one-room school often existed beside the local church. At school the young of farm laborers and village craftspeople learned the basics of reading, writing, and mathematics until they were ready to work in the fields or shops.

Students sat at benches with shelves in front serving as desktops and learned to pay attention, lest they be the victim of the teacher's ruler or stick. Educated women also established dame schools, where they gathered the village children in their homes to impart lessons in various subjects.

Until 1870 education for the poorer classes was even more haphazard, relying on schools for the poor set up by charities that offered the simplest of education. Since the families needed money, the income-producing capabilities of children was more important than sitting in a classroom. As a result, boys and girls of poorer families often went uneducated.

School generally lasted from 9:00 A.M. until 4:30 P.M., with a ninety-minute break in the middle for lunch and playtime. Two weeks at Christmas, another for Easter, and one month in the summer provided breaks for the students.

The universities, topped by Oxford and Cambridge, existed for the males from wealthy families who had attended one of the premier public schools. Students not only attended university for the education they received, but also for the connections they could make with sons of other prominent families. Oxford and Cambridge each contained separate colleges, some dating back to the 1200s, that focused on different subjects. Oxford built a reputation in literature and history, while Cambridge's acclaimed science curriculum drew students from across England. Later in the Victorian era, the University of London

Assassination Attempts

Occupying such a lofty position as a reigning monarch like Queen Victoria brings its rewards, but it also offers dangers that other citizens do not face. Three times in Victoria's first twelve years, she was the target of assassination attempts, as well as the object of a beating. On May 30, 1842, police arrested John Francis as he was about to fire a pistol at Victoria as she passed by in her carriage. Francis was found guilty of high treason and imprisoned for life. On July 3, 1842, John William Bean fired a pistol loaded with paper and tobacco, but no bullet, at Victoria. He was imprisoned for eighteen months.

In May 1849 William Hamilton fired at the queen's carriage as she rode through London, but like the first two attempts, he failed to cause any injury. According to a news account at the time, "Her Majesty heard the report [the pistol being fired] and looked round, but manifested no symptoms of alarm." Hamilton "was dragged off to the police station amidst the execrations [curses] of the crowd, who, if not for the activity of the police officers and others, would have executed Lynch law [hanging] upon the miscreant." Hamilton was found guilty of treason and imprisoned for seven years.

In June 1850 an ex-army officer, Robert Pate, attacked Victoria with a cane. She had again been in her carriage when Pate rushed up and struck her face. Though suffering a few bruises, Victoria emerged relatively unharmed. Pate, who many thought was insane, was also found guilty of treason and, like Hamilton, sent to prison for seven years.

http://www.newsletter.co.uk/news/local/queen_victoria_escapes_assassination_attempt_1_1885080

During her long reign, Victoria suffered many attempts on her life by would-be assassins, but all failed.

and other universities began rivaling the two premier institutions.

Females again took second place to males when it came to education. Few schools existed to educate women, mainly because English society in the early Victorian age did not see the need to do so. The wealthy used governesses to instruct their daughters through age twelve, with classes centering on proper manners and conduct.

That changed in the 1850s, when schools for girls became more commonplace. North London Collegiate School was the first to operate for girls, and within twenty years more such places appeared in other cities, including schools that offered courses in nursing and technology. Though Oxford and Cambridge established schools for females, women did not attain an equal footing with males in English education until the next century.

Educational Reforms

Pushed by reformers who argued that education was a right belonging to every child, and realizing that a connection existed between good education and an improved economy and workforce, Parliament eventually took steps. In 1862 it provided money for education and based the amount of money on how many students passed government-mandated standards of accomplishment in reading, writing, and mathematics.

The most influential change came in 1870 when a member of the House of Commons, W.E. Forster, persuaded Parliament to pass the Education Act, which required that education be made available to every child. Forster argued that not only was the act good for the welfare of the nation's children, it was also a way to ensure that England remained atop the world's industrial and technological powers. Forster said:

On the speedy provision of elementary education depends our industrial prosperity, the safe working of our constitutional system, and our national power. Civilized communities throughout the world are massing themselves together, each mass being measured by its force, and if we are to hold our position among men of our own race or among the nations of the world, we must make up for the smallness of our numbers by increasing the intellectual force of the individual.[49]

The law gave local authorities permission to raise taxes to fund schools and the power to enforce attendance for children who were either not working or attending another school. Separate rooms for each grade level became the norm. As a result, the children of poor and middle-class families learned new skills. Armed with enhanced education, they could look forward to better futures than before. While the new law did not solve every problem, it established the notion that the government had the duty to educate the nation's children.

The ensuing years saw more advances in education. An 1880 law made it mandatory for all children up to age ten to

Parliament passed the Education Act in 1870, requiring that every child get an education.

attend school, a revolutionary mandate that took children out of the workforce and placed them in schools. That same year the government established a board of education to supervise educational matters, and additional reforms in succeeding years raised the compulsory age to twelve and eliminated any costs to attend school.

Though some in the aristocracy objected, government intervention in different areas helped improve life for the majority. By the end of the century, people worked shorter hours and earned higher wages. Parents enjoyed a half day off on Saturday, every Sunday, and four holidays, during which time they could take weekend outings or attend sporting events. Children attended school rather than disappearing into mines and factories.

With some of the most basic needs now fulfilled, people in Victorian England could tend to other areas that needed improvement. They could also bring pastimes into their lives that filled the newly granted free time that came as a result of prosperity and government intervention.

Chapter Five

Life and Leisure in the Victorian Era

Because of the advancements achieved in the Victorian era and the prosperity that came with them, the English people enjoyed many improvements in their lifestyle over the course of the nineteenth century. Spurred by the same energy that caused businesspeople to build factories and railroads, city governments offered public parks, baths, and free libraries. Police departments made streets safer, and people lived longer because of advances in the medical field. A simultaneous increase in the number of people who owned their own homes gave workers in the Victorian era stability and a sense of pride.

Health and Medicine

Sweeping advances revolutionized the medical field. At the start of the Victorian era, most people failed to reach age fifty. Poor diets caused malnutrition and lessened the ability to fend off disease, and years of laboring in mines and factories produced ailments that led to early deaths. Poverty, overcrowding, and the lack of cleanliness in large cities proved fertile grounds for the rapid spread of diseases, and since physicians did not know that germs spread disease and thus failed to wash their hands after examining a patient, they carried disease from bed to bed.

The diets of the poor and working class, which consisted largely of bread, potatoes, cheese, and tea, led to stunted growth and weakened the ability to ward off disease. A series of epidemics ravaged the population. With physicians at first ignorant of the connection between germs and disease, sickness spread quickly in the overcrowded cities. One man who visited a city stricken with cholera, a deadly malady producing stomach pains, vomiting, and diarrhea that killed half of those who contracted it, wrote to his wife that it was no wonder that so many were in peril because of "the water of the common sewer which stagnated full of dead fish, cats, and dogs under their windows."[50]

One of the leading killers of the time, tuberculosis, also known as consumption, produced sweating, coughing, and loss of appetite. Four separate cholera epidemics between 1831 and 1866 killed 140,000 people. Typhoid, a disease spread by contaminated food or water, took the life of thousands, including that of Victoria's husband, Albert.

Death of a Prince

Albert fell ill in 1861 while tending to official and family duties. After inspecting the grounds of a new military academy at Sandhurst, Albert showed signs of fatigue. Three days later, while returning to Windsor Castle after a visit with his son at Cambridge, Albert caught a chill that worsened as the week went on.

Though he had been resolute in seeing to completion the Expedition of 1851 and in backing social reforms, Albert now showed little fight. "I do not cling

Britain's cholera epidemics overwhelmed medical science's, as well as the state's, ability to deal with them. This illustration depicts the crowded, unsanitary conditions in London slums that led to the outbreaks of cholera and other infectious diseases.

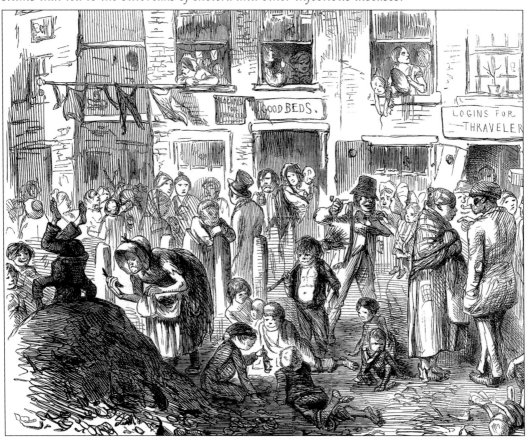

to life," he once told Victoria. "You do, but I set no store by it. I am sure, if I had a severe illness, I should give up at once, I should not struggle for life. I have no tenacity of life."[51] He even confided to a friend that he believed he would not recover from this recent illness. As he worsened, Victoria and her children spent more time with Albert. Princess Alice played tunes on the piano, and Victoria read to her husband.

Albert appeared better the morning of December 14 but deteriorated as the day wore on. Realizing that her husband was about to succumb, Victoria remained at his side, calmly staring at him. They exchanged pleasantries, and Albert kissed his wife on the forehead. Later that evening, the prince consort died.

"The Prince is dead," wrote the queen's treasurer, Charles Phipps, to Palmerston, the prime minister. "What will happen—where can she look for that support and assistance upon which she has leaned in the greatest and the least questions of her life?"[52]

For many years Victoria withdrew from public life. Without her beloved husband, she had little desire to appear at ceremonial functions. Instead, she spent most of her time at Windsor Castle or Balmoral Castle, a private estate she and Albert had purchased in Scotland.

Combating Disease

Victoria was not the only one who felt the loss of a loved one to disease. During the Victorian Era, thousands of mothers, fathers, husbands, and wives experienced similar events, and few families were untouched by one illness or another.

The epidemics had one beneficial result: They prodded medical science and the government to investigate the causes for the outbreaks. Rather than rely on the simple assumptions of the past, researchers studied diseases and attempted to discover scientifically sound reasons for their causes. That, in turn, led to their cures.

Government intervention yielded significant gains in battling illness. An 1842 paper, *Report on the Sanitary Condition of the Labouring Population*, was the first comprehensive survey of the nation's health. The investigators concluded that poor drainage, inadequate water supplies, and overcrowding helped cause poor health. The prominent physician John Simon chastised the government for its longtime neglect of the nation's health, writing, "This national prevalence of sanitary neglect is a very grievous fact" and called the delay in health measures "a worse than pagan savageness in the Christianity we profess."[53]

Use of anesthetics during surgery, which became more common after Victoria was placed under anesthesia for the births of her last two children in the 1850s, made procedures less difficult for the patient and increased survival rates. With better sanitation, the use of the anesthetic chloroform, and assistance by skilled nurses, hospital conditions improved. In the last quarter of the century, refrigeration enabled steamships and railroads to rush to market a more diverse selection of foods at a lower cost,

By the 1850s British hospital conditions had greatly improved, due to increased understanding of the need for sanitation, the use of surgical anesthetics, and implementation of standards and training for nurses.

making meats, fruits, and vegetables available to everyone. With an enhanced diet, life expectancy began to rise.

Positive Action

Reformers condemned the lack of a decent water supply as a prime contributor to poor health. Dr. John Simon, the author of an important 1890 book, *English Sanitary Institutions*, wrote that pure water was "the first essential of decency of comfort, and of health," but added that London had done little to provide such. Thousands of citizens lived in homes that lacked a water supply, which forced them, in Simon's words, to "depend on their power of attending at some fixed hour of the day, pail in hand, beside the nearest standcock [water pipe]; where, with their neighbors, they wait their turn—sometimes not without a struggle, during the tedious dribbling of a single small pipe."[54] A government commission pointed out that most every food product contained additives, "many of them injurious to health, and some of them even poisonous."[55]

As a result, the government took a more active role in regulating health and medicine and passed a series of laws designed to address health concerns. The Public Health Act of 1848 set up national and regional boards of health to ensure that minimum standards were followed. The act required that cities install more-efficient sewer systems, pipe in cleaner water, move slaughterhouses and cemeteries from residential areas, construct buildings with more ventilation and living space, have scheduled garbage collection, and provide school health examinations. The law also dropped the tax on soap in an effort to make it accessible to the poorest families.

In addition, Parliament passed laws that required vaccinations to eliminate epidemics and made bathrooms mandatory in buildings. The public gained increased respect for physicians when the government implemented a more rigid educational system to train doctors. A medical register was formed to list the licensed physicians, and a medical council enforced standards of practice.

Medical advances especially made significant headway in battling illness after Louis Pasteur and Joseph Lister published their theories in the 1860s. These two scientists had concluded that infections were caused by germs and that they could be prevented by washing hands and scrubbing medical instruments to kill germs. At first some physicians doubted the notion—they wondered how an organism so tiny could cause so much havoc. They dropped their objections, however, when the infection rates plummeted after doctors followed Pasteur's and Lister's advice and after the public, at the urging of government

health officials, began to bathe more frequently. By 1890 scientists had identified the bacteria that cause cholera and other diseases, and in the process the nation's health was vastly improved.

Police Departments

Similar improvements came in public safety, which at first was not seen as a government obligation. According to an 1818 Parliamentary report, organized police forces were unnecessary in fighting crime. A town or village only needed "the moral habits and opinions of the people,"[56] who by themselves could watch over their villages and towns and keep citizens safe. People hesitated to grant too much authority to a government police force, which might then be used by that government to suppress rights and liberties.

Instead, they relied on the system that had been in place since medieval times. Residents, according to the system, had a duty to police their own town and thus took their turn at patrolling the streets. In this fashion, each village not only kept a watch on crime, but also gave its residents a sense of accomplishment.

What might have worked in the Middle Ages, however, began to lack credence during the 1800s as metropolises started to grow. The expansion of cities and the widespread changes introduced into the country by industrialization heightened the situation. With thousands of people living in close proximity to one another, criminals had more opportunity to steal personal belongings. Fearing for their safety, people declined to enter certain parts of London, especially the slums of Bluegate Fields, Wapping Dock, and others. In some neighborhoods vigilante groups prowled the streets, offering a semblance of control but proving ineffective against criminals who roamed almost at will. Residents in wealthier neighborhoods barred their windows.

An 1822 government report concluded that criminals operated too freely and recommended the establishment of a police force in London and its suburbs. The Metropolitan Act of 1829 created such a unit for London. It divided the city into seventeen districts, each headed by a superintendent in charge of four inspectors and sixteen sergeants. Each sergeant in turn managed nine constables (police officers), with eight patrolling the streets and one operating out of the station house. The act proved so successful that Birmingham, Manchester, and other cities soon copied London.

Other improvements followed. In 1842 London's Criminal Investigation Department opened offices at Scotland Yard, which was charged with investigating the most serious crimes. It rapidly grew from two inspectors and eight sergeants to become one of the world's foremost crime-fighting organizations. By 1856 the government established standards for training police throughout the nation and assigned inspectors to ensure that local authorities implemented the standards.

Police forces throughout the Victorian era became more professional and effective. Edmund Henderson, the London police commissioner from 1868 to 1886, started compiling a register of

Punishment

Punishment could be severe in the Victorian era. Public executions were common until 1868 and drew enthusiastic crowds of people eager to witness the noose send another criminal to his or her final punishment. People often gathered the night before to ensure they had a good view of the hanging, spending the time drinking with others and singing songs until the execution occurred. Homeowners of residences near the execution made a profit off the affair by renting spots at their windows to eager spectators. This halted in 1868 when executions were moved behind prison walls.

Judges operated on the belief that prison was meant to punish and not to help the prisoner. They handed out lengthy prison terms including, in the early years of Victoria's reign, banishment to punishment colonies in distant Australia.

criminals and installed telegraphs in every police station. Beginning in 1895 the use of fingerprinting aided the police in identifying criminals. Combined with social reforms, better street lighting, and prosperity, police departments reduced crime rates as the 1900s neared.

Sports and Recreation

With increased incomes giving more people the ability to afford more than just the bare necessities, with government regulations reducing the number of hours a person worked each week, and with improved police departments offering enhanced security, families had more leisure time to devote to sports and other forms of entertainment. Team sports, with their emphasis on competition and the value of working together, especially appealed to the rising middle class. Through the Football Association in 1863, football (which is known in the United States as soccer) quickly became a favorite Saturday pastime for athletes and spectators. The Football League replaced the Football Association in 1885 and developed the worldwide game that soccer is today. Rugby, which allowed the use of hands and was more violent than soccer, also gained popularity. In 1880 the Amateur Athletic Association organized university and club championships in track and field, then sixteen years later helped form the first modern Olympic Games.

Sports clubs appeared in every major city and town. The All-England Lawn Tennis and Croquet Club started in 1869 and quickly became the ruling body for tennis. It held the first Wimbledon tournament in 1877, an event that has turned into one of the premier sporting contests in the world. Bare-knuckled boxing entertained many, but with critics calling the sport too bloody, in 1867 the Marquess of Queensberry compiled rules governing the sport. Boxers had to wear padded gloves to reduce injuries, and if a man could not rise after a count of ten, a referee halted the match rather than allowing it to go on until one man was unconscious.

The aristocrats favored hunting, racing, and croquet. Every June splendidly attired men and women attended the horse races at Ascot, while even Parliament shut down operations for Derby Day at Epsom Downs in late May or early June. The Oxford-Cambridge boat race in late March pitted teams from those two prestigious schools, while the Henley Regatta started its July tradition in 1839.

People of all social classes enjoyed the theater, dancing, archery, and visiting museums and zoos. They traveled to seaport resorts for brief respites from their work. Madame Tussauds wax museum in London drew thousands, and those who remained at home enjoyed games such as chess, backgammon, and charades. Starting in the 1850s bicycles and tricycles provided entertainment as well as a cheap method of transportation, and while the Victorian era predated the age of flight, spectators stared in awe at the occasional hot-air balloon that descended for a landing.

Everyone enjoyed music. Between 1850 and 1880, five hundred new music halls opened in London alone. At the

The first football (soccer) match between England and Scotland is depicted in this engraving. Football quickly became Britain's favorite Saturday pastime for athletes and spectators alike.

Savoy Theater, the first to install electric lighting, Gilbert and Sullivan thrilled audiences with their lively operas, many centering on duty and the impact of Britain on the world. The plays of William Shakespeare continued to draw large crowds, and puppet shows entertained young and old alike. The less wealthy flocked to halls that offered tickets at an affordable price to shows featuring singers, dancers, and comedians. As fashionable as these various forms of entertainment were, though, few rivaled the written word for popularity.

Dickens and Other Authors

Reading, from popular novels to newspapers and magazines, exploded in the Victorian era. Reforms in education handed book, magazine, and newspaper publishers a profitable market for the purchase of their goods, and changes in the workplace gave people more leisure time in which to read. Newspapers, such as London's *Daily Mail*, offered entertainment and features along with coverage of the nation's news, and they dropped their prices to where almost anyone could purchase the daily paper. In 1850

Jack the Ripper

One of the most infamous criminal cases during the Victorian era fascinates readers even today. In the autumn of 1888, several prostitutes were murdered in London's East End. The killer, also known as the Whitechapel murderer, slit their throats, then disemboweled the corpses, which indicated he may have had medical training. He sent notes to the police, almost as if he were daring them to locate him, and signed them "Jack the Ripper." Scotland Yard organized a widespread manhunt but failed to catch him.

The crimes remain unsolved. Authorities believed that the man killed five women over a ten-week stretch. One theory states that Victoria's grandson, Prince Edward, the Duke of Clarence, may have been involved to cover up knowledge of an affair. He supposedly had a child with a working-class girl that, if true, went against the prevailing customs. To end the rumors, someone murdered those who knew of the affair. Whether the grandson was involved in any way has never been determined, and any participation is based on speculation and rumor only. No charges were ever filed.

Other theories place the blame on Russian revolutionaries attempting to stir up trouble in the country. No definitive evidence has yet surfaced that would enable the police to state with certainty who the real Jack the Ripper was.

Parliament passed the Public Libraries Act, which started the trend away from libraries that charged a fee to use their collections—and thus limited books to those who could afford such items—to libraries that offered their collections free of charge. Heavy use of the railroads increased the desire for reading material to pass the time during long waits at stations and lengthy rides on trains. Stations even started libraries of their own, where passengers could pick up a book, read it during their ride, and deposit it at another library branch at the end of the trip.

The Victorian era produced some of the most impressive works of literature in modern history. Novelists and social critics vied with authors of fantasy and science fiction to satisfy the public's interest for new material.

Top on the list was Charles Dickens. Born in 1812, he had, before his death in 1870, published some of the most beloved works in literature. He introduced the fictional character Ebenezer Scrooge in *A Christmas Carol* in 1843, and made reading more accessible by offering some of his novels in serial form, with one section of a book appearing each month at a low cost. Families rushed to the stores to purchase the next installment of *Oliver Twist*, the tale of a young orphan, which appeared in monthly magazine sections from February 1837 to March 1839; *David Copperfield*, a semiautobiographical account of a young man, published in twenty different monthly parts of thirty-two pages each starting in May 1849; and *A Tale of Two Cities*, a novel about the French Revolution, published in sections from April to November 1859. Dickens thrilled the British public with some of the most memorable words in literature, from Scrooge's "Bah, humbug!" and Oliver Twist asking for more gruel to the opening lines of *A Tale of Two Cities*, "It was the best of times, it was the worst of times."[57]

Historical romance novels became wildly popular, especially books by the Brontë sisters. Emily Brontë's *Wuthering Heights*, first published in 1847, and sister Charlotte Brontë's *Jane Eyre*, published the same year, remain in print and have each been adapted by Hollywood into successful films several times.

Fantasy and Science Fiction

Lewis Carroll and Robert Louis Stevenson crafted two of the foremost books for young readers, who thrilled to fairy tales and adventure. *Alice's Adventures in Wonderland*, a delightful fantasy by Carroll, appeared in 1865. In it a young girl named Alice meets the White Rabbit, the Cheshire Cat, the Mad Hatter, and a host of intriguing characters in her odyssey into a different realm. In 1883 Stevenson penned *Treasure Island*, the yarn about a young boy named Jim Hawkins and his escapades with Long John Silver and his band of pirates on an idyllic ocean island. Three years later Stevenson followed with his tale of good versus evil in *The Strange Case of Dr. Jekyll and Mr. Hyde*. All have been the inspiration for film and television treatments long after they first appeared.

Other popular authors of the Victorian era turned to science and science fiction to educate or thrill audiences. In 1859 Charles Darwin presented the theory of evolution—that man evolved through millions of years from lower species of life and that only the strongest species survive—in his *On the Origin of Species*. Darwin's controversial notions created a public outcry, especially from those who believed in the biblical account of creation, led to a famous 1925 courtroom trial in the United States, and continue to appear in American politics in the twenty-first century.

At about the same time, H.G. Wells and Jules Verne used science fiction to predict what the future might hold as well as to entertain their readers. In 1895 Wells published *The Time Machine*, a novel in which his main character travels into the future. Two years later he wrote *The Invisible Man*, a tale about a scientist who invents a way to become invisible. In 1901, the year of Victoria's death, he came out with *The First Men in the Moon*, which predicted space travel. Wells later added other significant works, including *War of the Worlds*, after Victoria's death.

Though he was French, author Jules Verne entertained thousands in England. His science-fiction books, which included *A Journey to the Center of the Earth* (written in 1864), *Twenty Thousand Leagues Under the Sea* (written in 1870), and 1873's *Around the World in Eighty Days* predicted the widespread use of airplanes and submarines.

Praising the Nation

Two authors reflected the triumphs enjoyed by England during the Victo-

Lewis Carroll published his classic fantasy/satire Alice's Adventures in Wonderland *in 1865.*

rian era, both at home and throughout the world, in their writings. Arthur Conan Doyle introduced the fictional detective Sherlock Holmes in an 1887 novel, *A Study in Scarlet*. Basing Holmes on Doctor Joseph Bell, a renowned surgeon whose insightful diagnoses and treatments amazed his colleagues, Doyle fashioned a detective who relied on his vast intelligence, logic, and the use of modern forensic science to solve crimes. Holmes represented the triumph of the

Sherlock Holmes to the Rescue

Victorian England's most famous fictional detective, Sherlock Holmes, was resurrected in the 1940s to help England during her bitter battle against Adolf Hitler's Nazi Germany. In 1942's desperate days, when Hitler appeared on the verge of defeating England, two films appeared in British theaters, both designed to boost British morale. In *Sherlock Holmes and the Voice of Terror*, Holmes collects assistance from hardscrabble dockworkers to halt a Nazi plot inside the country. As the film ends and understated martial music wafts in the background, Holmes mutters to his faithful crony, Dr. Watson, an admonition that while trying times are yet to come, victory will be the result. Says Holmes, "There's an east wind coming Watson. Such a wind has never blown on England yet. It will be cold and bitter, Watson, and a good many of us may wither before its blast, but it is God's own wind nonetheless, and a greener, better, stronger land will lie in the sunshine when the storm has cleared."[1]

In the second film, *Sherlock Holmes and the Secret Weapon*, Holmes again foils an enemy plot, this time to steal an invaluable bombsight. A more positive Holmes, reflecting that England has withstood Hitler's worst, converses with Watson at the film's end as they stare out to sea beneath a canopy of British bombers on their way to blast targets inside Germany. "Things are looking up, Holmes," says Watson. "This little island's still on the map."[2]

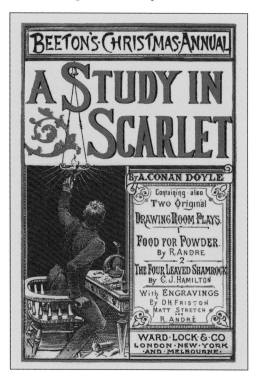

BEETON'S·CHRISTMAS·ANNUAL

A STUDY IN SCARLET

By A. CONAN DOYLE

Containing also
Two Original
DRAWING ROOM PLAYS.
1
FOOD FOR POWDER.
By R. ANDRE
2
THE FOUR LEAVED SHAMROCK
By C. J. HAMILTON

With ENGRAVINGS
By D.H. FRISTON
AND
MATT STRETCH
AND
R. ANDRÉ

WARD·LOCK·&·CO
LONDON·NEW·YORK
·AND·MELBOURNE·

1. *Sherlock Holmes and the Voice of Terror*. Directed by John Rawlins. Universal City, CA: Universal Pictures, 1942.
2. *Sherlock Holmes and the Secret Weapon*. Directed by Roy William Neil. Universal City, CA: Universal Pictures, 1943.

Sir Arthur Conan Doyle first introduced readers to supersleuth Sherlock Holmes in the 1887 novel A Study in Scarlet.

individual in the modern era, much as England had triumphed in industry, technology, and world affairs.

Teamed with his faithful cohort, Dr. Watson, Holmes pursued criminals in novels and short stories until 1893, when Doyle killed off the character in *The Final Problem*. The reading public raised such a cry that Doyle brought Holmes back for a lengthy run that lasted until 1927. Hollywood produced a string of Holmes films, starting in 1939 with *The Adventures of Sherlock Holmes* and *The Hound of the Baskervilles*, and continuing through 2011, when Robert Downey Jr. portrayed the detective in *Sherlock Holmes: A Game of Shadows*.

The second author became one of the most esteemed writers in history. Born in India in 1865, Rudyard Kipling reflected the prevailing attitudes held by people in the Victorian era—that England had the right to occupy the number one position among world powers and to enjoy the benefits that came with such a lofty position, as well as the duty to bring civilization—at least their brand—to what they considered the uncivilized parts of the world, especially India, the Middle and Far East, and Africa.

Kipling, who won the Nobel Prize for Literature in 1907, often wrote of English soldiers and the life of British citizens residing in India. His collection of short stories, especially *The Jungle Book* in 1894, introduced the mongoose Rikki-Tikki-Tavi and other popular figures, while his poetry spoke to the glories gained by heroic British soldiers and their Indian allies.

In the 1899 poem "The White Man's Burden," Kipling expressed this notion of the duty of the English soldier to serve in foreign posts and lift other people out of savagery and bring the advances of civilization to backward nations. On the other hand, in 1892 he penned "Gunga Din," a poem about a gallant Indian water bearer who saves a British soldier in the heat of bitter fighting. Though many British soldiers and civilians looked down on the Indian subjects they governed, Kipling ended his poem by having the saved British soldier proclaim that the Indian Gunga Din was the better man.

In their writings both Doyle and Kipling proclaimed the goodness of the British people. Kipling, especially, boasted of England's right to spread British civilization throughout the world. In the process the British under Victoria fashioned an empire that stretched to every portion of the globe, brought increasing fame and prosperity to London, and made Victoria respected and, in the form of her army and navy, feared.

Chapter Six

The Decline of Victorian England

The British Empire that existed in the mid- to late 1800s rivaled empires past, from Alexander the Great's Greek-dominated empire to the glories of ancient Rome. Diplomats and soldiers served in far-flung posts in an effort to impose the British way of life on others, and London hosted both European politicans and African chieftains. It was a grand time for England, but the glorious years also brought indignities and eventual decline to an empire that was so much a part of the Victorian era.

Imperialism

Imperialism, which was the desire to control other lands and acquire colonies throughout the world, was a cornerstone of British foreign policy from 1870 through the end of the Victorian era. It enjoyed widespread support in England, from the diplomats and soldiers to the factory owners and laborers. Economists saw a benefit in acquiring new lands and natural resources that, while adding to the glories of England, would also bring prosperity to poor and wealthy alike. Since France, Italy, and Germany also sought colonies, it became necessary to seize lands, even if for no other reason than to prevent the other nations from grabbing them. The British government kept a close watch on emerging European mainland powers, and possessing colonies and new markets was a way of checking the strength of a rival that could challenge British superiority. Finally, England could gain the world's respect, or at least its fear, by controlling large portions of the globe.

Benjamin Disraeli asked in 1872 whether the British people wanted "a comfortable England" or "whether you will be a great country, an imperial country, a country where your sons, when they rise, rise to paramount positions and obtain not merely the esteem of their countrymen but command the respect of the world."[58] They answered almost unanimously in favor of the latter.

England granted a degree of self-government to some of her colonies, such as Canada and Australia. Every colony, though, offered excitement and adventure to those who left home to serve the queen in foreign lands. Native people bowed to the queen's appointed representative, the governor, in India and elsewhere. British military commanders enjoyed respect at home and abroad, and British soldiers and sailors fought for the glory of Victoria and the acquisition of riches. The queen gained such immense popularity that in 1877 she was named the Empress of India, and her image rested in hundreds of locations, from a carved statue beneath a canopy of marble in India to a statue of the queen resting on a glorious throne on an Indian Ocean island.

Though the main reason England sought colonies was to benefit the nation, politicians and citizens alike proclaimed a more charitable motive—that in bringing British civilization to

A map of the world made near the end of Queen Victoria's reign shows the extent of the British Empire in red.

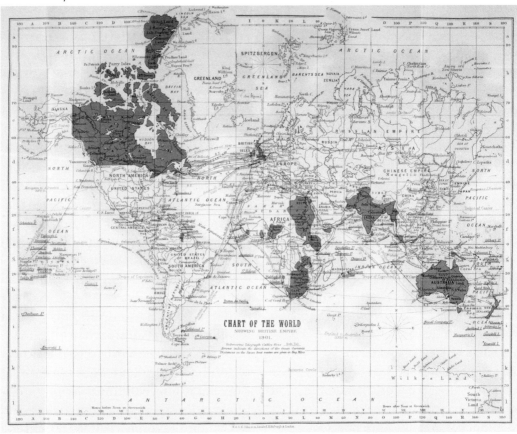

other lands, they would benefit those who supposedly lived in savagery. "It is because there are people like this in the world that there is an Imperial Britain," proclaimed the London *Daily Mail*. "This sort of creature has to be ruled, so we rule him, for his good and for our own."[59]

Few Britons disagreed with the sentiment. Businesspeople leaped at the opportunity to increase their profits, factory owners saw new markets for their products, soldiers jumped at the chance to gain glory in faraway lands, and missionaries responded to the opportunity to spread their religion to other lands. Rudyard Kipling wrote of new wonders and added powers, but warned that along with the glory came condemnation and hate from the people they attempted to help.

England grabbed other lands in so many places about the world that a journalist wrote, "the sun never sets upon the Union Jack [the nickname for the nation's flag]."[60] At its height, England commanded territory in five of the seven continents and islands off a sixth, leaving untouched only the frigid region of Antarctica. It governed widespread lands in Africa, both ends of the Mediterranean Sea, important lands in the Middle East, the entire Indian subcontinent, the region from Afghanistan to Thailand, various Pacific and Atlantic islands, Ceylon, Malaya, Singapore, Australia, and Canada. The British ruled one-quarter of the world's landmass and more than one-quarter of the world's population in an empire that was three times the size of the Roman Empire under Augustus Caesar and guarded by more soldiers than Julius Caesar commanded in ancient Rome. More than three hundred warships patrolled the world's sea lanes, keeping them open for British merchant vessels, and naval squadrons operated out of coaling stations in the Pacific, Atlantic, and Indian Oceans.

England acquired new lands so rapidly that the famous Victorian politician Lord Palmerston said he had to "keep looking the . . . places up on the map."[61] Much as New York City is in current times, London became the world's primary city.

Military Splendor

It was a heady time for the British military. People followed the exploits of armies and navies with newfound respect. Alfred Austin, England's poet laureate (the official poet for a country), claimed that for him, heaven would be sitting placidly in his garden listening to news of British victories on land and at sea. Poet W.E. Henley wrote that even severe wounds or death could not dampen the desire to expand the British way of life. Should any other nation contest England's right to acquire an empire, the English fell back on their military prowess and replied with an indifference that approached arrogance.

Schoolchildren thrilled to the stories of military glory and were taught that duty to the queen outranked every other quality. Stories emphasized loyalty and honor, and juvenile readers purchased

G.A. Henty's tales of soldiers in foreign lands as soon as they appeared on newsstands. Prints of popular paintings that depicted military feats adorned the walls of schools. Heroism in battle, even in a loss, was noble, while cowardice was unforgiveable. Students listened to the tale of Major Allen Wilson's last stand on the banks of Africa's Shangani River in Africa. During fighting against the Matabele warriors, Wilson and his thirty-two soldiers, out of ammunition after an exhausting struggle, shook hands, stood shoulder to shoulder, and sang "God Save the Queen" as the Matabele fighters closed in and slaughtered them.

When in 1880 twelve soldiers died covering the retreat of a British brigade, Garnet Wolseley, who commanded forces in Africa and India, wrote of the band's commanding officer, "I envy the manner of his death. If I had ten sons, I should indeed be proud if all ten fell as he fell."[62]

The Crimean War

England took pride in the many wars, small and large, in which its forces became involved. In March 1854 England declared war on Russia after that nation sent troops to occupy certain sections of Turkey. The British government wanted to maintain access to the Christian holy land, which it feared Russia might sever, and believed that England had a duty as a world power to help prevent Turkey from being overrun by Russia.

British forces invaded the Crimea, a peninsula in southern Russia, and quickly besieged their opponent at Sevasto-

pol. The siege, which lasted more than a year, gave Russia the chance to organize counterattacks against the British. The combat included one charge conducted near the village of Balaclava, immortalized by Alfred, Lord Tennyson, in his poem "The Charge of the Light Brigade" after British cavalry galloped into almost certain death by riding directly into enemy gunfire.

The yearlong stalemate caused shortages of weaponry and supplies among the British expedition, which battled hunger and inadequate medical facilities while fighting the Russians. Mistakes by untested field commanders complicated matters. Since newspaper correspondents covering the war were able to relay information rapidly back to England, the public avidly followed developments. William H. Russell of the *Times* and other correspondents wrote of the troops' sufferings and their lack of supplies, causing outrage in England. The government adopted steps to improve the flow of supplies and asked nurse Florence Nightingale to establish a nursing corps in the Crimea. She and her nurses made such significant strides in tending the wounded that nursing became an admired profession in England.

Even the queen became involved. After visiting a group of wounded soldiers in February 1855, Victoria wrote in her journal, "I cannot say how touched & impressed I have been by the sight of these noble, brave, & so sadly wounded men & how anxious I feel to be able to use them, & to try & get some employment for those who are maimed for life."[63]

France and Turkey allied with Britain to defeat Russia in the Crimean War in the mid-1850s but at an enormous cost to the British government and with little prestige gained for the empire.

The queen often met with Nightingale to find the best solution to aid those who had been injured in the war. On September 21, 1856, they talked for two hours, during which time Nightingale discussed the deficiencies of the military hospital system in impressive style. "We are delighted with her great gentleness, simplicity and wonderful, clear head,"[64] wrote Victoria. She established a commission to determine ways to improve conditions for soldiers, including hospital conditions, which was the first time the government conducted such an investigation into life for a soldier.

The Crimean War ended in March 1856 with the Treaty of Paris. Although England gained little prestige from a war that claimed the lives of twenty-one thousand British soldiers, the reforms encouraged by the correspondents and enacted by Nightingale made the military better able to face future clashes.

The Indian Mutiny

England had hardly ended her battle with Russia when she became embroiled in strife in India. Long considered the jewel of the British Empire, India had been associated with England since the 1600s, when the East India Company established a trade presence there.

Upset about rumors that cartridges for a new rifle had been greased with the fat of cows, animals that Hindus considered holy, in January 1857 three regiments of Indian troops mutinied. Others around the nation soon joined, igniting the widespread slaughter of English families as well as of soldiers.

The deaths, especially those of women and children, shocked England and forced the government to employ troops to quell the mutiny. Victoria wrote in her journal on July 1, 1857, that there were "such sad accounts from India, the mutiny among the native troops spreading, sad murders of Europeans at Meerut, still worse at Delhi." She later wrote to King Leopold of Belgium, "We are in sad anxiety about India, which engrosses all our attention. Troops cannot be raised fast, or largely enough. And the horrors committed on the poor ladies—women and children—are unknown in these ages and make one's blood run cold."[65] She informed Leopold that few families had not been affected by the loss of someone in India.

The poorly organized mutiny ran out of steam when it encountered British forces under Hugh Rose. Within a year conditions in India had returned to normal, and the British government decided to take a more active role in ruling the country. Through the years England sent some of its most prominent diplomats to the nation, where, families in tow, they governed the subcontinent in splendor for their queen.

Africa and the Far East

Since newspaper correspondents covered the mutiny in detail, the British public not only read of the fighting but also learned of exotic cities and lands, all under the control of England. This increased the desire for additional colonies. In the late 1880s much of Africa had been unexplored by European countries, but within twenty years a handful of nations, including England, had moved in. Using superiority in modern weaponry, British forces overcame Egyptian resistance and captured Cairo, intent on digging the Suez Canal through that nation to shorten the long journey from England to India and the Far East.

England also added the Sudan and South Africa, where the British battled the fierce Zulu warriors, to its list of colonies. The fighting against the Zulus handed schoolchildren one of Britain's most stirring military actions when in January 1879, 139 British troops commanded by Lieutenant John Chard successfully defended the small British post at Rorke's Drift against 4,500 Zulu warriors. Eleven Victoria Crosses, the nation's highest military honor, were bestowed on members of the defense at Rorke's Drift. English forces later pushed into Nigeria, the Congo, and Zanzibar.

In 1884 Gladstone sent one of the country's most famous commanders, General Charles Gordon, who had helped crush a rebellion in China in the 1860s, to evacuate British garrisons threatened by a massive native uprising in the Sudan. England experienced a bitter defeat in January 1885 when Sudanese troops surrounded the city of Khartoum and massacred Gordon and his eleven thousand troops.

Thirteen years later a British army commanded by General Horatio Herbert Kitchener defeated the Sudanese

During the Zulu War of 1878–1879, a British force of 139 men successfully defended Rorke's Drift against forty-five hundred Zulu warriors.

and recaptured Khartoum. Winston Churchill, a young officer who would later gain fame as England's prime minister during World War II, wrote of the fighting that "discipline and machinery triumphed over the most desperate valour, and after an enormous carnage, certainly exceeding 20,000 men, who strewed the ground in heaps and swathes 'like snowdrifts,' the whole mass of the Dervishes [Muslims] dissolved into fragments and into particles and streamed away into the fantastic mirages of the desert."[66]

England also entered the Pacific Ocean and Far East. In 1858 it joined other European nations in seizing Chinese forts and two years later swept into Peking. The Europeans forced the Chinese government to grant concessions, including allowing the presence of British, French, and Italian military forces.

Burma and Malaysia in the Far East soon fell to British forces. Victoria's forces went on to seize Pacific Ocean islands, including Papua and the Solomon Islands, to use as coaling stations for her fleet or to guard the approaches of important locations such as Australia. Before the end of the century, England had planted its flag and governed colonies around the world.

First Signs of Decline

England had enjoyed decades of prosperity and achievement under Victoria. As the century neared an end, however, signs of decay began to appear. The first came in nearby Ireland. Fiercely independent, the Irish wanted the repeal of the Act of Union of 1800, which combined Great Britain and Ireland. Many Irish detested being under British rule and demanded what they called home rule, or government by their own prime minister and parliament.

Gladstone realized that retaining Ireland might be more trouble than it was worth and twice introduced bills in Parliament requesting home rule for the country. The House of Commons rejected the first attempt in 1886, which led to rioting in Belfast that killed many citizens. Parliament also voted down a second attempt in 1893. By the end of the Victorian era, the issue still had not been decided. The problem, however, showed that not everyone viewed British rule as a blessing.

Meanwhile, across the globe in China, resentment built among the Chinese toward the presence of foreign nations, including Great Britain. Bitter feelings had existed between Britain and China since the first of two wars over trading rights in China had flared in 1839. The British handily defeated their foe, receiving in return Hong Kong and trading rights. Along with the French, Italians, and other nationalities, the British operated from a portion of Peking called the International Settlement. They relied on military advantages to maintain their dominance over the weaker Chinese government.

The presence of foreign armies in China's midst gave birth to a secret society called the Righteous Harmonious Fists, called the Boxers by the Europeans. The Boxers demanded the expulsion of all foreigners, along with the Chinese who had converted to Christianity, and resorted to violence when their calls went unheeded. When the Boxers burned homes and attacked missionaries throughout 1898 and 1899, Britain and other powers sent almost five hundred sailors and marines from eight nations to protect their interests and citizens in Peking.

When the Boxers attacked in June 1900 and besieged the European portions of Peking, a British diplomat requested additional relief. The combined countries organized a joint military force of more than two thousand men under the command of Admiral Edward Seymour, a British officer, to protect their citizens. The Boxers attacked and halted Seymour before he reached Peking, forcing him to turn back.

The allied nations next assembled a force of twenty thousand men, this time under the command of a German officer, which began marching toward Peking in August. This detachment battled its way through Chinese opposition, reached the foreign settlements in Peking, and lifted the siege. The turmoil ended when the Chinese government signed a peace treaty that abolished the Boxers.

Though England maintained its footing in China into the next century, the Boxer Rebellion showed how feeble Britain's stand was in that nation. Simmering Chinese resentment could at any moment lead to another native association to challenge British supremacy. England also lost prestige in that, after a British officer failed, a German officer successfully commanded the relief expedition. It was another sign that, in the later years of Victoria's tenure, power was slipping to other countries.

The Boer War

England's decline accelerated with the Boer War of 1899 to 1902. The affair began when gold discoveries in the late 1880s in South Africa caused thousands of foreigners, mostly British, to pour into the region. The local authorities, called the Boer government, placed restrictions on the newcomers because they feared that Great Britain, bolstered by the presence of so many English, would try to take over South Africa.

A failed attempt by British horsemen to cause an uprising of native residents and overthrow the Boer government worsened matters. When the German ruler, Kaiser Wilhelm II, telegraphed his congratulations on foiling the uprising to the Boer president, the British government became alarmed. They feared that Germany, a fast-rising nation on the European mainland, had intentions of intervening in South Africa. When the Boer government refused a British demand for better treatment of Britons in South Africa, hostilities started.

The war opened poorly for England when Boer forces, supported by German guns and artillery officers, issued three defeats in seven days. News of the losses at Magersfontein, Stormberg, and Colenso stunned the British. Unaccustomed to seeing their supposedly superior forces so badly manhandled, the British labeled the period the "Black Week."

Charles Gordon

Charles "Chinese" Gordon was one of the most popular, and controversial, military commanders of the Victorian era. Born January 28, 1833, Gordon entered the military in 1852. He served with distinction in the Crimean War and in fighting against the Chinese, where he picked up his nickname. In 1873 he was named the governor of Equatoria in the Sudan, Africa, where he quashed the slave trade. After a brief time in England, in 1884 Gordon returned to the Sudan to evacuate troops from the Khartoum area, but for another year they were besieged by the forces of Muhammad Ahmad al-Mahdi. On January 26, 1885, Ahmad's units broke into Khartoum and slaughtered the defenders, including Gordon.

According to legend, Gordon supposedly changed into his dress uniform and stood at the top of a flight of stairs to wait for the Sudanese. When they approached the stairs, the Sudanese paused at seeing the famous leader before one soldier shouted that Gordon's time had come. The British leader turned away in scorn moments before a volley of spears killed him.

Two days later a British relief column reached Khartoum, too late to help the besieged forces. The British public acclaimed the slain commander as "Gordon of Khartoum" and blamed the government for not sending the relief force sooner, but there is evidence that Gordon may have ignored orders to leave Khartoum while he could still evacuate his troops.

In the legend of Charles "Chinese" Gordon at Khartoum in Africa, Gordon faced down Ahmad's soldiers just before his death.

When the Boers then besieged three other British-held towns, Britain dispatched additional forces under Earl Roberts of Kandahar, who lifted the sieges and captured the Boer capital. Kitchener, who had enjoyed success in Africa, was brought in to complete the fighting but faltered against Boer tactics. For two years a frustrated Kitchener tried to engage his opponent in a large-scale battle, but the Boers successfully relied on hit-and-run attacks to harass the British. In an effort to locate his foe, Kitchener destroyed homes, crops, and buildings, and placed men, women, and children in detention camps surrounded by barbed wire. His tactics gained Britain the condemnation of many nations, as well as a growing number of British citizens, who saw the desperate moves as a sign that Great Britain could not humanely solve the crisis.

Kitchener eventually gained the upper hand, however. The Boer government finally yielded in early 1902 when British forces entered the capital. Relieved that the fighting was over, Britain granted additional independence to the Boers in a peace settlement and agreed to help rebuild the towns and cities that had been destroyed.

Much as the Vietnam War would do to the United States later in the century, the Boer War earned the strong disapproval

Winston Churchill in Africa

The man who gained great distinction in successfully leading Great Britain against Adolf Hitler in World War II (1939–1945) gained his first military training during the Victorian era. As a young officer, Winston Churchill served in the Sudan and participated in the momentous Battle of Omdurman on September 2, 1898, in which British forces defeated the Sudanese who had taken Khartoum from Charles Gordon.

Lined up that day with the twenty-six thousand British soldiers who faced forty thousand Sudanese was Winston Churchill. Two days later he described the battle in a letter to his mother, Lady Randolph Churchill. "I was under fire all day and rode through the [cavalry] charge," he explained. He fired his pistol ten times, killing five men, but fortunately escaped harm. He added that the Sudanese slashed with their swords and fired their rifles from a few feet away, and "showed no fear of cavalry and would not move unless you knocked them over with the horse."

Randolph S. Churchill. *Winston S. Churchill, vol. 1, Youth, 1874–1900.* Boston: Houghton Mifflin, 1966, p. 400.

of other countries and disillusioned many British citizens. Rather than pursuing a noble cause, critics argued that man's desire for gold had caused a war costing the lives of twenty-two thousand British and seven thousand Boer soldiers, plus an additional twenty thousand women and children who perished in the camps. Many British citizens began to question imperialism and wondered whether the yearning for colonies was either worthwhile or morally proper. Unlike past conflicts, and unlike the achievements that marked industrialization and technology, the Boer War shook British confidence and indicated that Victorian England was on the decline.

The German Threat

As the century waned, England basked in glories that had been largely attained from past achievements. In 1887 the nation celebrated Victoria's Golden Jubilee (fifty years on the throne). Victoria marked the occasion by hosting an elaborate feast attended by fifty princes and kings. Ten years later the nation again staged festivities as Victoria marked her Diamond Jubilee (sixty years). The *Daily Mail* printed a special edition all in gold. A member of the British Empire, Canada, printed a postal stamp that contained a map of the world with Britain's far-flung possessions colored in red and the words, "We hold a vaster Empire than has been."[67]

Besides the Boer War, other signs indicated that England's long prominence was coming to an end. Other countries in Europe and elsewhere, particularly the United States, assembled industrial machines that rivaled England's, thereby ending her long dominance in that area. On the European mainland, Germany had already placed itself in a prime position to challenge England by handily defeating France in the Franco-Prussian War of 1871.

Concern on the part of British politicians intensified when Germany began to build a fleet of ships. Already the premier land force on the continent, should Germany possess a navy to rival England's navy, that nation could disrupt England's lines of communication to India and other places in its world empire and threaten English control of the sea.

British leaders had a right to be alarmed. In 1899 a German adviser asked the German kaiser when he might be ready to challenge England militarily. Wilhelm responded that for the time being, he had to use restraint. "I am not in a position to go beyond the strictest neutrality, and I must first get for myself a fleet. In twenty years' time, when the fleet is ready, I can use another language [employ his guns rather than his words]."[68] When Gladstone visited Germany and saw the construction of new battleships, he said, "This means war!"[69]

The End of the Victorian Era

Though war did not come during the Victorian era, both leaders were correct. In 1914 the two nations declared war in a strife that eventually embroiled Europe and the United States in World War I.

Hundreds of thousands of people lined the streets of London to watch Queen Victoria's funeral procession on January 28, 1901. Historians mark her death as the official ending of the era that bears her name.

That, however, rested in the future. The Victorian era came to its official end with the queen's death. Weakened from rheumatism and plagued by poor eyesight from cataracts, the eighty-one-year-old monarch passed away on January 22, 1901. British citizens and politicians boasted of the nation's accomplishments under the queen and looked ahead with a confidence that, while shaken by more recent events, had carried England through the early years of industrialization and on to the main stage of world dominance.

One day after the queen died, the *Times* of London summarized what Victoria had meant to the country. The editorial said that the era "has been one of intellectual upheaval, of enormous social and economic progress, and, upon the whole, of moral and spiritual improvement. It is also true, unfortunately, that the impetus has to some extent spent itself. At the close of the reign we are finding ourselves somewhat less secure of our position than we could desire." The newspaper added, though, that the progress made under

Victoria could yet remain the cornerstone of England's future.

If we now enter upon our work in the spirit embodied in the untiring vigilance and the perpetual openness of mind that distinguished the Queen, if, like her, we reverence knowledge and hold duty imperfectly discharged until we have brought all attainable knowledge to bear upon its performance, her descendants will witness advance not less important than that of her long and glorious reign.[70]

Lady Salisbury, the wife of the prime minister, may have summed it up best. When discussing how people would remember the Victorian era, she said, "The young generation may criticize us as they like; will they ever provide anything as good as what we have known?"[71]

Notes

Chapter One: Technology and Industrialization

1. Quoted in Sally Mitchell. *Daily Life in Victorian England*. Westport, CT: Greenwood, 2009, p. 4.
2. Quoted in Cecil Woodham-Smith. *Queen Victoria: Her Life and Times*. London: Book Club Associates, 1973, p. 246.
3. Quoted in Lytton Strachey. *Queen Victoria*. New York: Harcourt, Brace, 1921, pp. 302–303.
4. Quoted in G.M. Young. *Victorian England*. London: Oxford University Press, 1936, p. 96.
5. Quoted in Anthony Wood. *Nineteenth Century Britain, 1815–1914*. London: Longmans, Green, 1960, p. 105.
6. W.J. Reader. *Victorian England*. London: William Clowes, 1973, p. 17.
7. Quoted in Reader. *Victorian England*, p. 16.
8. Quoted in Reader. *Victorian England*, p. 17.
9. Quoted in E. Royston Pike. *"Golden Times": Human Documents of the Victorian Age*. New York: Schocken, 1967, p. 41.

Chapter Two: The Splendor of Victorian England

10. Quoted in Woodham-Smith. *Queen Victoria*, p. 373.
11. Quoted in Pike. *"Golden Times,"* p. 27.
12. Quoted in Pike. *"Golden Times,"* pp. 32–33.
13. Quoted in Pike. *"Golden Times,"* p. 45.
14. Quoted in Woodham-Smith. *Queen Victoria*, pp. 376–377.
15. Quoted in Reader. *Victorian England*, p. 96.
16. Quoted in Pike. *"Golden Times,"* p. 57.
17. Quoted in J.F.C. Harrison. *The Early Victorians, 1832–1851*. New York: Praeger, 1971, p. 16.
18. Quoted in William Manchester. *The Last Lion: Winston Spencer Churchill*. Boston: Little, Brown, 1983, p. 60.
19. Quoted in Pike. *"Golden Times,"* pp. 85–86.
20. Quoted in Reader. *Victorian England*, p. 34.
21. Quoted in Manchester. *The Last Lion*, pp. 72–73.
22. Reader. *Victorian England*, p. 24.
23. Quoted in Geoffrey Best. *Mid-Victorian Britain, 1851–1875*. New York: Fontana, 1971, p. 272.
24. Quoted in Wood. *Nineteenth Century Britain, 1815–1914*, p. 112.
25. Quoted in Hilary Evans and Mary Evans. *The Victorians: At Home and at Work*. Newton Abbot, Devon, Great Britain: David & Charles, 1973, pp. 17–18.

Chapter Three: The Abuses of the Era

26. Quoted in Reader. *Victorian England*, p. 86.
27. Quoted in Harrison. *The Early Victorians, 1832–1851*, p. 26.
28. Quoted in Reader. *Victorian England*, p. 105.
29. Quoted in Reader. *Victorian England*, p. 79.
30. Quoted in Reader. *Victorian England*, p. 104.
31. Quoted in Pike. *"Golden Times,"* p. 72.
32. Quoted in Harrison. *The Early Victorians, 1832–1851*, p. 18.
33. Quoted in Pike. *"Golden Times,"* pp. 64–65, 69–70.
34. Quoted in Pike. *"Golden Times,"* p. 71.
35. Quoted in Wood, *Nineteenth Century Britain, 1815–1914*, p. 116.
36. Quoted in Reader. *Victorian England*, p. 63.
37. Quoted in Harrison. *The Early Victorians, 1832–1851*, p. 39.
38. Quoted in Reader. *Victorian England*, p. 60.
39. Quoted in Harrison. *The Early Victorians, 1832–1851*, p. 27.
40. Quoted in Wood. *Nineteenth Century Britain, 1815–1914*, p. 116.
41. Quoted in Reader. *Victorian England*, p. 116.
42. Quoted in Peter Quennell, ed. *Mayhew's Characters*. London: William Kimber, 1951, p. 84.
43. Quoted in Quennell. *Mayhew's Characters*, pp. 158–159.

Chapter Four: Victorian Era Reforms

44. Quoted in Quennell. *Mayhew's Characters*, p. xix.
45. Quoted in Wood. *Nineteenth Century Britain, 1815–1914*, p. 124.
46. Quoted in Reader. *Victorian England*, p. 115.
47. Quoted in Reader. *Victorian England*, pp. 67–68.
48. Quoted in Manchester. *The Last Lion*, p. 79.
49. Quoted in Young. *Victorian England*, p. 115.

Chapter Five: Life and Leisure in the Victorian Era

50. Quoted in Wood. *Nineteenth Century Britain, 1815–1914*, p. 121.
51. Quoted in Strachey. *Queen Victoria*, p. 293.
52. Quoted in Woodham-Smith. *Queen Victoria*, p. 505.
53. Quoted in Pike. *"Golden Times,"* pp. 273–274.
54. Quoted in Pike. *"Golden Times,"* p. 279.
55. Quoted in Pike. *"Golden Times,"* p. 296.
56. Quoted in E.L. Woodward. *The Age of Reform, 1815–1870*. Oxford: Clarendon, 1938, p. 447.
57. Charles Dickens. *A Tale of Two Cities*. Mineola, NY: Dover, 1999, p. 1.

Chapter Six: The Decline of Victorian England

58. Quoted in Gordon A. Craig. *Europe Since 1815*. New York: Holt, Rinehart and Winston, 1966, p. 448.
59. Quoted in Manchester. *The Last Lion*, p. 53.
60. Quoted in Manchester. *The Last Lion*, p. 44.
61. Quoted in Manchester. *The Last Lion*, p. 45.
62. Quoted in Manchester. *The Last Lion*, p. 55.

63. Quoted in Woodham-Smith. *Queen Victoria*, p. 418.
64. Quoted in Woodham-Smith. *Queen Victoria*, p. 441.
65. Quoted in Woodham-Smith. *Queen Victoria*, pp. 450, 453.
66. Quoted in Craig. *Europe Since 1815*, p. 467.
67. Quoted in Reader. *Victorian England*, p. 212.
68. Quoted in Wood. *Nineteenth Century Britain, 1815–1914*, p. 385.
69. Quoted in Wood. *Nineteenth Century Britain, 1815–1914*, p. 385.
70. Quoted in Young. *Victorian England*, p. 170.
71. Quoted in Barbara Tuchman. *The Proud Tower*. New York: Macmillan, 1966, p. 58.

For More Information

Books

Geoffrey Best. *Mid-Victorian Britain, 1851–1875*. New York: Fontana, 1971. Best examines the middle years of Victoria's reign, focusing on the impact of railroads, the rise of the middle class, and education and religion in the country.

Randolph S. Churchill. *Winston S. Churchill*. Vol. 1, *Youth, 1874–1900*. Boston: Houghton Mifflin, 1966. The author, who was the son of the famous British prime minister who is the subject of the book, relies heavily on letters and other writings of his father to deliver a complete account of his father's early life.

Gordon A. Craig. *Europe Since 1815*. New York: Holt, Rinehart and Winston, 1966. This outstanding history of Europe in the nineteenth century and beyond provides a clear summary of the events that marked Victoria's reign.

Hilary Evans and Mary Evans. *The Victorians: At Home and at Work*. Newton Abbot, Devon, Great Britain: David & Charles, 1973. The authors wrote a lively account of life during the Victorian era that includes chapters on education, labor, health, and communications.

J.F.C. Harrison. *The Early Victorians, 1832–1851*. New York: Praeger, 1971. Harrison shows what daily life was like for people during the first part of Victoria's reign.

William Manchester. *The Last Lion: Winston Spencer Churchill*. Boston: Little, Brown, 1983. Manchester's superb biography of Great Britain's heralded prime minister includes an outstanding section showing life in the Victorian era.

Sally Mitchell. *Daily Life in Victorian England*. Westport, CT: Greenwood, 1996. Mitchell offers one of the best surveys of life during Victoria's reign. She shows how the various classes differed and how science and reform helped alter the country.

Sally Mitchell, ed. *Victorian Britain*. New York: Garland, 1988. Mitchell's nine-hundred-page encyclopedia offers information on the people, events, and daily lives for individuals in the Victorian era. The comprehensive summaries provide a fascinating look at one of Great Britain's most prominent eras.

Jan Morris. *The Spectacle of Empire*. Garden City, NY: Doubleday, 1982. Morris writes of the British Empire under Victoria. Readable text is supported by numerous photos that help bring that era alive.

E. Royston Pike. *"Golden Times": Human Documents of the Victorian Age*. New

York: Schocken, 1967. Pike collects an informative array of newspaper articles, government testimonials, and other sources to depict life in England during the Victorian era.

Peter Quennell, ed. *Mayhew's Characters*. London: William Kimber, 1951. Quennell has gathered some of the most dramatic accounts of London's poor collected by Henry Mayhew, who investigated the matter and wrote of it in the 1850s.

W.J. Reader. *Victorian England*. London: Clowes, 1973. Reader focuses on how people lived and how the Victorian era affected the different social classes. He emphasizes the contributions of the emerging middle class.

Lytton Strachey. *Queen Victoria*. New York: Harcourt, Brace, 1921. Strachey's readable prose helps give a fascinating portrait of the dominant figure of her times.

Barbara Tuchman. *The Proud Tower*. New York: Macmillan, 1966. One of the most respected historians, Tuchman surveys the Victorian era in this history of Europe in the last quarter of the nineteenth century.

Anthony Wood. *Nineteenth Century Britain, 1815–1914*. London: Longmans, Green, 1960. Wood's book offers a balanced look at events that occurred both in England and throughout the world.

Cecil Woodham-Smith. *Queen Victoria: Her Life and Times*. London: Book Club Associates, 1973. One of the best biographies of the queen, Woodham-Smith relies heavily on Victoria's let-

ters and her journal to present a sympathetic portrait.

E.L. Woodward. *The Age of Reform, 1815–1870*. Oxford: Clarendon, 1938. Eminent historian Woodward delivers a wide-ranging summary of England on the eve of the Victorian era and during the era's first half.

G.M. Young. *Victorian England*. London: Oxford University Press, 1936. This overview of Victoria's reign contains helpful summaries of various social and political events.

Websites

British Monarchy (www.royal.gov .uk/historyofthemonarchy/king sandqueensoftheunitedkingdom/ thehanoverians/victoria.aspx). This is the official website of the British monarchy. It is filled with information about every king and queen and contains portions of Victoria's journal.

Charles Dickens, Goodreads (www .goodreads.com/author/quotes/239 579.Charles_Dickens). This website contains hundreds of favorite quotes from Charles Dickens.

Kipling Society (www.kipling.org .uk). The website for the Kipling Society contains a wealth of information on the famous English author. The site has links to other locations, plus reprints of most of Kipling's works.

Victorian Web (www.victorianweb .org/index.html). This website contains information about the Victorian era, including technology, science, and authors.

Index

in 1845, *29*
establishment of police force in, 72
growth of, 28
neighborhoods of, 30–31
unsanitary conditions in, *68, 70*
London Labour and the London Poor (Mayhew), 56

M
Macaulay, Thomas Babington, 26
Married Women's Property Acts (1870, 1882), 62
Mayhew, Henry, 27, 51, 56
Medicine, advances in, 69, *70*, 71
Metropolitan Act (1829), 72
Middle class
    rise of, 36, 38
    social reform and rise of, 85
Military, 9, 82–83
    careers in, 38
    Kipling's writings on, 79
Monarchy, 21
Music halls, 73, 75

N
Napoleon Bonaparte, 9, 11
Newspapers, 75
Nightingale, Florence, 83, 84

O
Oliver Twist (Dickens), 76
On the Origin of Species (Darwin), 77
Orphanages, 59
Oxford University, 63

P
Palace of Westminster (Houses of Parliament), 30
Palmerston, Lord, 35–36, 82
Parliament, 21
Pasteur, Louis, 71
Paxton, Joseph, 26
Phipps, Charles, 69
Pickpocketing, 53
Police departments, 71–73
Poor Law Amendment Act (1834), 59
Postal system (penny post), 16, 33–34
Poverty/the poor, 39–40, 67
    attitudes about, 55

Dickens' focus on, 56
farmworkers and, 48–49
reforms targeting, 58–59
Public Health Act (1848), 71
Public Libraries Act (1850), 75–76

Q
Queensberry, Marquess of, 73

R
Railroads, 18–20
    growth of cities and, 32–33
    national unity and, 20–22
Recreation, 73, 75
Reform Bill (1867), 61
Reforms
    in education, 62–63, 65–66
    impetus for, 55–56
    targeting children/the poor, 58–59
    in voting system, 59–60
    in worker's rights, 60–61
Report on the Sanitary Condition of the Labouring Population, 69
Righteous Harmonious Fists (Boxers), 87–88
Rocket (steam engine), 19
Roman Empire, 82
Rorke's Drift, 85, *86*
Rose, Hugh, 85
Rugby, 73
Russell, William H., 83

S
Sale of Food and Drug Act (1875), 58
Salisbury, Lady, 93
Salt, Titus, 45
Saltaire textile factory, 45, *45*
Sanitary conditions
    disease outbreaks and, 69
    improvements in, 33, 58, 70–71
    in London, *68*
Self-Help (Smiles), 27
Seymour, Edward, 88
Sherlock Holmes, 77–79
Sherlock Holmes and the Secret Weapon (film), 78
Sherlock Holmes and the Voice of Terror (film), 78
Simon, John, 69, 70

Picture Credits

About the Author

John F. Wukovits is a retired junior high school teacher and writer from Trenton, Michigan, who specializes in history and biography. Besides biographies of Anne Frank, Booker T. Washington, Michael J. Fox, Eli Manning, and Martin Luther King Jr. for Gale, he has written biographies of the World War II commander admiral Clifton Sprague, Barry Sanders, Tim Allen, Jack Nicklaus, Vince Lombardi, and Wyatt Earp. He is also the author of many books about World War II, including *Pacific Alamo: The Battle for Wake Island*; *One Square Mile of Hell: The Battle for Tarawa*; and *Black Sheep: The Life of Pappy Boyington*. A graduate of the University of Notre Dame, Wukovits is the father of three daughters—Amy, Julie, and Karen—and the grandfather of Matthew, Megan, Emma, and Kaitlyn.